Lessons Experimental Translators Can Learn from *Finnegans Wake*

Inspiring translators by making specific experimental writing strategies available to them, this book reimagines experimental translation through close readings of *Finnegans Wake*.

Robinson's engagement with translational aspects of *Finnegans Wake* provides rich and useful insights into experimental translation that encourage new approaches to translation theory and practice. The author analyses Joyce's serial homophonic translations, portmanteau words, and heteronyms along translational lines (following Fritz Senn, Clive Hart, Patrick O'Neill, and others), and offers a showcase translation of Walter Benjamin's "Task of the Translator" using all three experimental techniques borrowed from the *Wake*.

The book will be a valuable addition to any postgraduate course in translation theory, literary theory, and Joycean literature. Translation scholars, students, and researchers will find this text a compelling read.

Douglas Robinson is a prolific scholar, with three dozen books, seven dozen articles and book chapters, and numerous book-length translations from Finnish into English. He has taught all over the world, including the University of Mississippi, the University of Jyväskylä and the University of Tampere in Finland, Lingnan University, and Hong Kong Baptist University. Upon his official retirement in 2020 he became Emeritus Professor of Translation, Interpreting, and Intercultural Studies at Hong Kong Baptist University and Professor of Translation Studies and Head of the Division of Intercultural Communication at the Chinese University of Hong Kong (Shenzhen).

Routledge Advances in Translation and Interpreting Studies

Audio Description and Interpreting Studies
Interdisciplinary Crossroads
Edited by Cheng Zhan and Riccardo Moratto

Gendered Technology in Translation and Interpreting
Centering Rights in the Development of Language Technology
Edited by Esther Monzó-Nebot and Vicenta Tasa-Fuster

Emerging Englishes
China English in Academic Writing
Alex Baratta, Rui He and Paul Smith

A Bergsonian Approach to Translation and Time
Toward Spiritual Translation Studies
Salah Basalamah

Self-Care, Translation Professionalization, and the Translator's Ethical Agency
Ethics of *Epimeleia Heautou*
Abderrahman Boukhaffa

Lessons Experimental Translators Can Learn from *Finnegans Wake*
Translouting that Gaswind into Turfish
Douglas Robinson

For more information about this series, please visit: www.routledge.com/Routledge-Advances-in-Translation-and-Interpreting-Studies/book-series/RTS

Lessons Experimental Translators Can Learn from *Finnegans Wake*

Translouting that Gaswind into Turfish

Douglas Robinson

LONDON AND NEW YORK

First published 2025
by Routledge
4 Park Square, Milton Park, Abingdon, Oxon OX14 4RN

and by Routledge
605 Third Avenue, New York, NY 10158

Routledge is an imprint of the Taylor & Francis Group, an informa business

British Library Cataloguing-in-Publication Data
A catalogue record for this book is available from the British Library

ISBN: 9781032746869 (hbk)
ISBN: 9781032746890 (pbk)
ISBN: 9781003470427 (ebk)

DOI: 10.4324/9781003470427

Typeset in Times New Roman
by Newgen Publishing UK

Thanks to Legenda for permission to reprint two images from Clive Scott's *Translating the Perception of Text.*

Thanks to the University of Toronto Press for permission to quote from Patrick O'Neill's *Polyglot Joyce.*

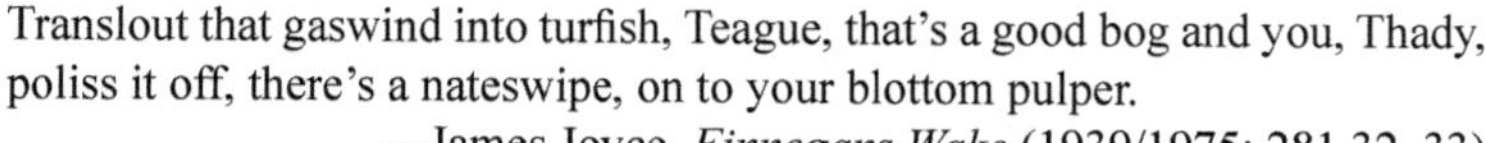

Translout that gaswind into turfish, Teague, that's a good bog and you, Thady, poliss it off, there's a nateswipe, on to your blottom pulper.

—James Joyce, *Finnegans Wake* (1939/1975: 281.32–33)

Contents

1	Preface: How To Do Things With *Finnegans Wake*	1
2	Translouting into Djreamish	18
3	Heteronymous Translouters	47
4	A Showcase of Joycean Experimental Translation: "Benjamins Totin' Vodka"	65
5	Postface: Translouchewality	104

Appendix *121*
References *127*
Index *134*

1 Preface: How To Do Things With *Finnegans Wake*

Let's begin with the line in *Finnegans Wake* that I've set as my epigraph, and from which I take my subtitle: "Translout that gaswind into turfish, Teague, that's a good bog and you, Thady, poliss it off, there's a nateswipe, on to your blottom pulper" (*FW* 281.32-33).

What can we do with that?

1a

The obvious first thing we can try to do is to *understand* it. That is the task served by the dozens of glossaries that scholars have prepared for the *Wake*: unpack Joyce's multilingual portmanteau words so that we can understand each sentence and paragraph and chapter "properly."

But then many Joyce scholars have challenged that assumed "propriety"—the notion that to read the *Wake* with understanding we have to understand exactly how each polyglot coinage works, which is to say we have to be able to break each apart into its multilingual semantic ingredients.

"Just read it," these protestors say. "Read it for the music."

Or: "Read along and let the meanings of the words emerge gradually as you go."

But that kind of advice goes against the grain of all our education as "smart" people. We have been trained to figure things out, to delve deeply into the heart of complex sentences in search of the key to it all.

Once we have that key, we—what?

Well, we have arrived. We can be taken seriously as scholars. We're not just faking it; we're the real thing.

DOI: 10.4324/9781003470427-1

1b

That is almost certainly the motivation those dozens of scholars have felt to research and write all those glossaries: Joyce is a great writer, well worth the effort we must expend to understand him; *Finnegans Wake* is one of the most difficult reads in world literature; "delving deeply" seems to require extensive etymological research; I have the kind of requisite specialist knowledge of one or more of the sixty-odd languages from which Joyce built his coinages in the *Wake*; I'll do my fellow scholars a great service, and track down *all* the words that draw on that language or those languages that I know.

1c

To put that demystifyingly: literature professors gravitate to difficult literary classics because mastering them elevates them (us) to a kind of secular priesthood. It is deeply gratifying to know that people rely on our ability to interpret and explain the secular sacred text.

Expertise in say Robert Frost doesn't yield that kind of gratification. Any reasonably articulate high school student can do an expert reading of "The Road Not Taken" or "Stopping by Woods on a Snowy Evening."

The difficult task of reading a work like *Finnegans Wake* propels not only students but English department colleagues with other specializations to seek out the Joycean who can explain the *Wake*. They *need* us.[1] The arcane knowledge we possess bestows an intensely prestigious kind of cultural capital on us (among the handful of people who really want to read the *Wake*).

1d

Faced with "Translout that gaswind into turfish," then, we can begin by pushing hard on our own knowledge of English, or check English dictionaries.

Even without foreign-language glossaries, we either know or can easily find out that a lout is a rude and violent person or an awkward hayseed, and so can guess that "translout" could mean something

1 I'm not really including myself in this "us." I'm very much a novice at the *Wake*. My first-person plural here is a hypothetical expansion of the small band of Joyceans as exemplars of literature professors in general (and I do belong to that latter group).

like "translate loutishly," or "translate what louts write," or "treat this source text as written by louts," or "translate this for louts."

We can read "poliss" as "polish" or "Polish," but also as "police."

Any English dictionary will tell us that "nates" are buttocks, borrowed from the Latin; a "nateswipe" could thus be either a "buttocks wipe" or a "buttock swipe."

"Blottom" seems to be composed of "blot" and "bottom," and a pulper is obviously a machine for reducing fruit or paper-stock or other matter to pulp; "blottom pulper" also sounds vaguely like "blotting paper."

1e

And then of course once we've worked through the English echoes, we can scour the glossaries for foreign sources.

"Lout" is pronounced exactly like German *laut*, which is "loud" or "noisy" as an adjective, means "sound" or "noise" when capitalized as a noun, and is used prepositionally for something like "according to." In Early High German *laut* was one conjugation of the verb *lauten* "to sound, to ring"—but that is an obsolete sense that nowadays has shifted into something like "to read": *der Brief lautet* is "the letter reads," which is to say implicitly something like "the words in the letter when read aloud sound like this." So "translout" thought through German would have an embodying effect on reading, or translating-as-reading: translating the sounds of the words, or homophonic translation (sections 2d-h); translating sounds or noises even without words.

"Gaswind" also points us to German: the adverb *geschwind* means "quickly." Translout that gaswind quickly.

"Turfish" sounds a bit like "Turkish"—translate that gaswind quickly into Turkish—but for an Irishman like Joyce (and "Teague" is a nickname for an Irishman) it would also hint at the idiom of Ireland, the land of turf.

"Bog" is not just marshy ground (in English and French) but "soft" or "flabby" in Irish and Scottish Gaelic, "book" and "beech" in Danish and Norwegian *nynorsk*, "shoulder" in Swedish and Norwegian *bokmål*, "knot" in Hungarian, "bent" in German, and "god" (and various figurative extensions, such as "paragon" or "highest value") in many Slavic languages. In Old English it was the spelling of Modern English "bough," and also meant a plant's sprig and (as in Scandinavian languages) the arm or shoulder.

"Thady" seems to be Thaddeus, according to apocryphal tradition the name of Jesus's brother. In Christian theology Thady would be bog's baby brother.

"Nateswipe" draws not only on a Latinate asswipe but another German phrase as well, *nett's Weib* ("nice woman").

And German glossaries for the *Wake* suggest that "pulper" also seems to suggest the German noun *Pulver* (powder).

1f

Fritz Senn (2013: 135) writes of Issy's footnote in which the "translout that gaswind" line appears:

> A footnote is appended to the quotation: *Translout that gaswind into turfish* (*FW* 281). It appropriately deals with translation; whether it is into Turkish or Irish (Ireland is the country of turf), it leaves open. German *laut* « loud » and *geschwind* « quickly » add yet another local colour, and the result may be nothing but gas and wind.

Does that help?

1g

The interpretive method tracked in sections 1d-e seems like an extraordinarily labor-intensive way to read a 600-page novel, of course. And since this is ultimately a book not about *Finnegans Wake* but about experimental translation, we would probably be forgiven if we decided *not* to read all 600 pages in that manner, but were simply, say, to read this one line as about translation.

So now again: "Translout that gaswind into turfish, Teague, that's a good bog and you, Thady, poliss it off, there's a nateswipe, on to your blottom pulper."

Fritz Senn says fairly noncommittally that the line "appropriately deals with translation." But deals how?

1h

Read as a characterization of "translation," perhaps, the line seems quite churlish—far more aggressively dismissive of translators and translations than Senn's detached "deals with translation" would seem to warrant.

Translators are louts—or else they are people who busy themselves with the words or sounds emitted by louts.

Those words or sounds, the contents of the source text, are "gaswind."

"Turfish" would seem a quite demeaning term for a target language: turf is sod, dirt covered with grass, or maybe a block of peat cut out of the soil to be used as fuel, arguably making "turfish" the language of people who pull on their slops (rough baggy trousers) to go out onto the bog to dig up peat for their stoves.

And once the translator has polished/policed the translation and sent it off, it would seem to be demeaned as mere toilet paper or blotting paper. (And in Chapter II-3 we hear the story of "Buckley and the Russian General," a story Joyce's father loved to tell, about an ordinary Irish soldier who decides not to shoot a Russian general he has in his sights, because the general clearly has gastric issues, and drops his trousers to defecate; but when the general grabs a clod of turf to wipe his nates, Buckley takes offense and shoots and kills him.)

1i

But is it really as offensive a take on translation as it seems to be?

Joyce was not, of course, theorizing translation, let alone writing a manual for experimental translators. He was writing an experimental novel.

True, it might be argued that in writing *Finnegans Wake* Joyce was himself translating the waking English of the 1864 Irish-American street ballad "Finigan's Wake"—

> Tim Finigan liv'd in Walker Street,
> an Irish gentleman mighty odd
> He'd a beautiful brogue so rich and broad
> And to rise in the world he carried the hod
>
> https://repository.duke.edu/dc/hasm/b1044

—into an invented djream polylanguage sleepily embedded in English:

> Bygmester Finnegan, of the Stuttering Hand, freemen's maurer, lived in the broadest way immarginable in his rushlit toofarback … and during mighty odd years this man of hod, cement and edifices in Toper's Thorp piled buildung supra buildung pon the banks for the livers by the Soangso.
>
> *FW* 4.18-28

And every word of that target djream polylanguage was supposed to enable "three score and ten toptypsical readings" (*FW* 20.15)—an experimental explosion of what might be considered translational potential.

1j

But apart from all that, what we are doing with the translouting line is now not understanding it as Joyce intended it to be read but figuring out what *we* can do with it. We are not tracking Joyce's themes but thematizing in our own right, imposing our own themes on Joyce's novel.

But in any case, even if Joyce did intend that line to be a slur on translation, it would have been a *local* slur. It is a footnote written by Isobel/Isabel/Isolde/Issy at the foot of a page that her twin brothers (Dolph/Shaun and Kev/Shem, whom she nicknames "Teague" and "Thady") are studying and annotating in the lesson that is Chapter 2 of Part II, encouraging one or both of them to translate a sentence in French from Edgar Quinet's introduction to his 1827 French translation of Johann Gottfried von Herder's *Ideen zu Philosophie der Geschichte der Menschheit* ("Ideas on the Philosophy of the History of Humanity," written between 1784 and 1791), with cryptic notes in the left margin written by Shem and the right written by Shaun:

Twos Dons Johns Threes Totty Askins. *Also Spuke Zerothruster.*	*Aujourd'hui comme aux temps de Pline et de Columelle la jacinthe se plaît dans les Gaules, la pervenche en Illyrie, la marguerite sur les ruines de Numance*[1] *et pendant qu'autour d'elles les villes ont changé de maîtres et de noms, que plusieurs sont entrées dans le néant, que les civilisations se sont choquées et brisées, leurs paisibles générations ont traversé les âges et sont arrivées jusqu'à nous, fraîches et riantes comme aux jours des batailles.*[2]	THE PART PLAYED BY BELLETRISTICKS IN THE BELLUM-PAX-BELLUM. MUTUOMORPHO-MUTATION.

[1] The nasal foss of our natal folkfarthers so so much now for Valsinggiddyrex and his grand arks day triump.

[2] Translout that gaswind into turfish, Teague, that's a good bog and you, Thady, poliss it off, there's a nateswipe, on to your blottom pulper.

1k

Richard Ellmann (1959/1982: 664) translates the Quinet quotation like this: “Today as in the time of Pliny and Columella the hyacinth disports in Wales, the periwinkle in Illyria, the daisy on the ruins in Numantia and while around them the cities have changed masters and names, while some have ceased to exist, while the civilizations have collided with each other and smashed, their peaceful generations have passed through the ages and have come up to us, fresh and laughing as on the days of battles.”

Does that implicitly/retroactively hail Ellmann as Isobel’s turfish-nateswipe translouter?

Does it hail him at one remove as “Teague” or “Thady”?

And does it help?

1l

Joyce scholars have ascertained that Joyce loved this quotation, had memorized it, used it in conversation, and here misquotes it slightly. It is the *Wake*’s only extended quotation in the original non-English language, and as we’ll see in sections 1p-u it appears in various forms throughout the novel and gives significant shape to the novel.

Joyce scholars have also told us that Joyce didn’t actually read Quinet’s sentence in the introduction to his translation of Herder but found this passage in March, 1924, in Léon Metchnikoff’s *La civilisation et les grands fleuves historiques*—and that Metchnikoff was in fact the one to misquote it.

We also learn from the scholars that reading Metchnikoff was the turning point or tipping point for Joyce in imagining the *Wake*; Metchnikoff was the source of Joyce’s heavy structural and historical reliance on Giambattista Vico’s cyclical theory of history, *corsi* and *recorsi*, historical courses and recurrences, or what Joyce’s narrator early on calls “a commodious vicus of recirculation” (*FW* 3.2).

Does that help?

If you want to read more on this passage, check out the 2017 blog posts by Cameron McEwen (“Bellum-Pax-Bellum”) and Peter Chrisp (“Edgar Quinet in Finnegans Wake”). Neither, however, dips into the “translout[ing of] that gaswind into turfish.”

1m

The point in sections 1j-l is that that second footnote to the Quinet quotation is not a universalizing summation of translation but a situated moment in a long difficult novel.

We are the ones generalizing it as a derogatory theory of translation (section 1h).

We are the ones who (in sections 1g-l) can't be bothered to transpose the semantic tracking from sections 1d-e to the whole novel, and are instead inclined to cut our losses and put the line to good (?) purpose as a general theory.

1n

But sections 1a-m are only ways of getting us started. As my title suggests, I am primarily interested here in "Lessons Experimental Translators Can Learn from *Finnegans Wake*."

In other words, rather than *understanding* the line (and others like it) thematically as a guide to either Joyce's novel or translation, I propose to *take practical advice* from it on how to do experimental translation.

As I specifically put the question in my chapter title and brief introductory paragraph, the issue is not *what is this?* or *what does this mean?* but *what can we do with it?*

1o

This book had its beginning in an earlier book I wrote on avant-garde translation: *Translator, Touretter: Avant-garde Translation and the Touretter Sublime* (Robinson 2024b). There I developed a model for avant-garde translation based on Jonathan Lethem's strategy in *Motherless Brooklyn* to mobilize the narrator's Touretter tics as a gateway for insinuating "Joycean wordplay" into a realistic novel—and for examples of Joycean wordplay I went to *Finnegans Wake*.

That is to say: (a) *Wakean* wordplay as a model for (b) literary Touretter tics as a model for (c) avant-garde translation. So now, I thought in envisioning *Lessons*, why not simply cut out the b-middleman? In that previous book I had explored that Touretter middleman at length, and just barely dipped into *Finnegans Wake*; that offered an obvious sort of progression from *Touretter* to *Translouter*.

Incidentally, it was a discussion of Jonathan Lethem's *Harper's* article "The Ecstasy of Influence" (2007) in my previous book *The Experimental Translator* (2023c: 65-67, 71-73) that reminded me of *Motherless Brooklyn*; and once I started exploring the sublime for the *Touretter* book I began to explore Longinus's theorization of ecstasy as "being driven out of yourself."

From *Experimental* to *Touretter* was not as obvious a progression as from *Touretter* to *Translouter*, maybe, but does display some kind of imagistic continuity nevertheless.[2]

1p

If Joyce translated obsessively throughout the *Wake*, and indeed if the *Wake* as a whole can plausibly be read as an extended djream translation, the obvious first place to look for lessons experimental translators might learn from the novel would be the novel's own translations.

A good starting place might be Clive Hart's account of Isobel's second footnote to Quinet and its follow-ups:

> Isobel writes two footnotes to Quinet, in the second of which she suggests that the flatus of his very spiritual style be transmuted into the rather more solid matter to be found on Anna Livia's cloacal scrap of tissue:[3]
>
> "Translout that gaswind into turf, Teague, that's a good bog and you, Thady, poliss it off, there's a nateswipe, on your blottom pulper."
>
> Joyce takes Isobel's advice and parodies the [Quinet] sentence in five places in *Finnegan's Wake,* thus "translouting" it into his Irish "turfish" and thoroughly assimilating it into the book. (I have used the word "parody" here for want of a better. Joyce is not really parodying Quinet at any point, but refashioning his sentence word by

2 For another novelistic experiment in Joycean wordplay, see my *Insecticide: A Republican Romance* (2024a), where the excuse to indulge in *Finnegans Wakean* portmanteau word play is the dyslexic word salad of George Bush father and son, the 41st and 43rd presidents of the United States, who narrate the novel.

3 Hart footnotes this with "Cf. the Russian General's cleaning himself with a sod of Irish turf (353.15)."

> word to suit new contexts—an altogether different art for which no adequate term seems to exist. The five "parodies" are more like free translations into various dialects of "Djoytsch").[4]
>
> Hart 1962: 188

"No adequate term," right: but perhaps "experimental translation" would work?

Hart takes a more pointed stance on the tonal attitudinalization of Isobel's "translout" footnote than Senn: "she suggests that the flatus of his very spiritual style be transmuted into the rather more solid matter to be found on Anna Livia's cloacal scrap of tissue." It doesn't just "deal with translation": it deals with translation as shit.

But it's also clear from his analysis that "Joyce takes Isobel's advice," which is to say that Joyce is only playfully dragging (his own experimental) translations in the mud. It's not really a churlish smear (perfunctory apologies for that pun).

1q

Here are two of the "five places" Hart mentions, after a reminder of the opening of Quinet's sentence:

> *Aujourd'hui comme aux temps de Pline et de Columelle la jacinthe se plaît dans les Gaules, la pervenche en Illyrie, la marguerite sur les ruines de Numance* [...]

> While Pliny the Younger writes to Pliny the Elder his calamolumen of contumellas, what Aulus Gellius picked on [...]
>
> *FW* 255.19-20

> [...] since the days of Plooney and Columcellas when Giacinta, Pervenche and Margaret swayed over the all-too-ghoulish and illyrical and innumantic in our mutter nation [...]
>
> *FW* 615.2-4

4 "Djoytsch" is Hart's Joycean portmanteau of "Deutsch" (German) and "Joyce" (and "joy"): joyful Joycean German, presumably pronounced "joych." Of course German is only one of five dozen languages out of which Joyce builds his portmanteau "djream" polylanguage. (I have I imported the "dj" spelling from Hart's Djoytsch to "djream," with the added benefit that DJR are my initials.)

There Joyce is mainly just rejoycing the French, enjoyceably but fairly superficially rendering Pline as Pliny the Elder and Plooney, Columella as a "calamolumen of contumellas" and Columcellas, *la jacinthe* as Giacinta, *les Gaules* as Aulus Gellius and "all-too-ghoulish," *la pervenche en Illyrie* as "picked on" and "Pervenche … illyrical," *la marguerite* as Margaret, *Numance* as "innumantic," and so on.

1r

Elsewhere he goes farther, digs deeper:

> Since the days of Roamaloose and Rehmoose the pavanos have been strident through their struts of Chapelldiseut, the vaulsies have meed and youdled through the purly ooze of Ballybough, […] those danceadeils and cancanzanies have come stimmering down for our begayment […]
>
> *FW* 236.19-21, 28-30

There all the personal and place names have been changed not slightly and playfully but radically: the Roman authors Pliny and Columella have become the "Roamin" authors "Roamaloose" (Romulus) and "Rehmoose" (Remus), and the flower theme has been petalodied out into a dancing-flower theme. "Pavanos" are elaborately dressed dancers (the name of the dance comes from *pavus*, Latin for peacock), "vaulsies" are French *valses* "waltzes," "purly ooze" is *purlieus* (the "outlying areas" where villagers would gather to dance), "danceadeils" are daffodils rethought through dance and the devil ("deil"), "cancanzanies" are obviously zany versions of the cancan, and so on.

1s

A side note: "Mr Frank Budgen insists that Joyce detested flowers, and indeed even the graceful periwinkle, hyacinth and daisy of Quinet's sentence are prized more for the abstractions they embody than for their sensuous qualities" (Hart 1962: 186).

Hart is eloquent on Joyce as an urban author who was not much interested in nature, except for the Liffey, which, he says, was not so much "nature" as it was part of Joyce's urban environment in Dublin.

The "purly ooze of Ballybough," now an inner-city district of Dublin, was still semirural when Joyce lived in the city; it was first settled in 1605, but the oozy sloblands along the Liffey estuary left "Mud Island" (as it was called them) at the mercy of the sea, and until land reclamation happened in the twentieth century the inhabitants were all poor and lived in mud houses.

1t

Joyce found the Quinet quote in 1924, and two years later, in 1926, he wrote the first chapter of *Finnegans Wake*, and encapsulated that chapter's prehistory of Dublin in a (roama)loose translation of the Quinet:

> Since the bouts of Hebear and Hairyman the cornflowers have been staying at Ballymun, the duskrose has choosed out Goatstown's hedges, twolips have pressed togatherthem by sweet Rush, townland of twinedlights, the whitethorn and the redthorn have fairygeyed the mayvalleys of Knockmaroon, and, though for rings round them, during a chiliad of perihelygangs, the Formoreans have brittled the tooath of the Danes and the Oxman has been pestered by the Firebugs and the Joynts have thrown up jerrybuilding to the Kevanses and Little on the Green is childsfather to the City (Year! Year! And laughtears!), these paxsealing buttonholes have quadrilled across the centuries and whiff now whafft to us, fresh and made-of-all-smiles as, on the eve of Killallwho.
>
> *FW* 14.35-15.11

In a very real sense, in fact, by proliferating experimental translations of the Quinet quotation throughout the novel Joyce was not just "thoroughly assimilating it into the book" but making it an embedded microcosm (a *mise en abîme*) of the novel: Quinet's cyclical *paisibles générations [qui] ont traversé les âges et sont arrivées jusqu' à nous, fraîches et riantes comme aux jours des batailles*, or "peaceful generations [that] have passed through the ages and have come up to us, fresh and laughing as on the days of battles," have become "these paxsealing buttonholes [that] have quadrilled across the centuries and whiff now whafft to us, fresh and made-of-all-smiles as, on the eve of Killallwho," a dance of the flowers lasting a thousand years ("chiliad of perihelygangs" or a millennium of around-the-sun-goings)—and of course the last five letters of "chiliad" allude to the *Iliad* as the first war epic.

"Killallwho" refers to the Battle of Clontarf in 1014 CE, in which the Irish King Brian Boru defeated the Danes and so ended the Viking invasions of Ireland (King Brian's stronghold was at Killaloe).

Those "buttonholes" that have sealed the peace by "quadrill[ing] across the centuries" have been dances of war-peace-war, or, in Shaun's right-margin note, "BELLUM-PAX-BELLUM."

1u

The Viconian cyclical conception of time that Joyce borrowed from Metchnikoff/Quinet as the temporal framework of the novel means that there is no beginning, no middle, and no end to the *Wake.* Various stories recur, get retold from different perspectives, with new twists that interrupt them, divert them, reshape them; and the novel's last sentence famously circles back around and continues in its first. (See sections 2u-z for a discussion of Jacques Lacan's aggrieved reading of that broken or fractalized cyclicality.)

As Joyce wrote to his patron Harriet Shaw Weaver in 1926, "One great part of every human existence is passed in a state which cannot be rendered sensible by the use of wideawake language, cutanddry grammar and goahead plot" (quoted in MacCabe 1982/2016: 24): the *Wake* is a djream narrative in which nothing is experienced first-hand, story comes to us piecemeal at second or third hand, through rumors and vague obfuscatory denials, and nothing is ever resolved. No "wideawake language," no "cutanddry grammar," no "goahead plot."

The fact that the Quinet quotation is a *mise en abîme* of the novel *in French*, and Joyce's experimental translations of that *mise en abîme* into what Clive Hart calls "Djoytsch" disseminate its wager of hyperabyssality from the first chapter ("Since the bouts of Hebear and Hairyman") to the last ("since the days of Plooney and Columcellas"), arguably makes the whole novel an experimental translation …

… and therefore useful as a model for experimental translation—or, as I propose to couch it in this book, for translouting into djreamish.[5]

Maybe. We'll see.

5 As noted earlier (p. 10, note 4), I base the portmanteau coinage "djream(ish)" on Clive Hart's coinage "Djoytsch"—but also on the "signature" fact that DJR are my initials.

1v

This might be a good place to stop and ask the elephant-in-the-living-room question: not just *why translout into djreamish*—why explore or indulge experimental translation—but *what we can learn from Joyce's novel about possible* ***reasons*** why we might want to translout into djreamish.

One approach to that question might be to ask what Joyce hoped to get out of writing the way he did, "djreamishly"; another might be to ask what the *Wake*'s fans get out of it.

In fact, given the remarkable difficulty of reading the book, these questions are often raised by Joycean scholars.

Philip Kitcher (2009: 41–42), for example, treats them this way:

> Joyce described his book in many ways, including some of what we can reasonably take to be his favorite characterizations within the book itself. One that occurs relatively late suggests that it is a gift, a "beautiful crossmess parzel" (619: 4-5). Overtly hostile (or cross) readers might focus on the "mess," but a more benign reaction would take Joyce simply to have set us a gigantic puzzle, a lifetime's worth of the most ingenious, taxing, and witty cryptic crosswords. Many people who become enamored of the *Wake* effectively treat it in this way, concentrating on this passage or that, exploring the many possible puns, finding a touch of Sanskrit here or Kigali there, uncovering an allusion to Irish legend or Egyptian burial rituals, tracing a connection to a popular song of the 1890s or a sign in the window of a Dublin merchant. This activity can be enormous fun, and it is, of course, perfectly harmless. Yet if this is all that can be made of the *Wake*, then the admirers of *Ulysses* who worried that Joyce was wasting seventeen years of his life were right; the great setters of crossword puzzles have done as much (and with less sacrifice).

By the same token, one of the lessons experimental translators might learn from the *Wake* should probably *not* be that gratuitous lexical complication is an end in itself—probably not that it might be somehow deeply rewarding to astound and even overwhelm target readers with one's vocabularian creativity.

Then what?

1w

Consider this: a traditional realistic novel is based tacitly on the assumption that life, experience, engagement with the world is fully conscious and subject to control by the rational mind. The narrator makes sense of that world, so that readers can understand everything that happens in the novel, even when the characters don't. The narrator is the author's explainer stand-in for the reader—the author's rational avatar, as it were.

In the same way, a traditional equivalence-based translation is based tacitly on the assumption that translation too is a purely rational activity. There is a source text that is eminently sensible, written in full rational consciousness by the source author and subject to (near-)perfect control by the target reader's rational mind. The translator makes target-language sense of that text, so that target readers can understand everything that the source author intended. The translator is the source author's rational stand-in for the target reader.

1x

In writing a (post)modernist djream novel, Joyce set himself in opposition to that whole premodern set of assumptions about novels. We do not have full rational control over our engagement with the world. The Freudian unconscious, the world of dreams, shapes everything we do in weirdly irrational ways. We want things without realizing that we want them, and without realizing the extent to which that unconscious wanting prestructures our experience of the world. "Reality" comes to us not just mediated but disturbingly distorted by the unconscious. (Arguably this makes experimental novels like *Ulysses* and *Finnegans Wake* exemplars of a new kind of realism.)

And now ask yourself whether translating is as rational and rationally controllable an activity as traditional thinking about it would like us to believe. Is it possible to exhaust by rational means not only our understanding of the source text but the interpretativity of our mediation process? Do we really know everything we need to know about how the relevant words and phrases in both the source and target languages are used by different people, in different genders and social classes and ethnicities and workplaces and other subcultures? Do we have full control of our stylistic choices? Do we even have a full and reliable grasp of the cognitive regimes we bring to bear on managing the complexity of the stylistic choices we make? Do we understand our own textual and stylistic analyses, or our (holizing) constructions of (fractal) synonymity? Do we have intimate cognitive and affective knowledge of every possible future target reader that our translation may someday have?

Isn't it plausible that the Freudian unconscious, the world of dreams, shapes everything we translators too do in weirdly irrational ways?

If so, isn't "translouting into djreamish" a *realistic* response to that state of affairs?[6]

1y

A slightly less buoyant take on that shift would follow Jacques Lacan (again, see sections 2u-z) in mobilizing historicizing accounts of the "rationalist" understanding of fiction and translation as putative ("commonsensical," Enlightenment) "sanity" and any Freudian or other antirationalist understanding as "insanity."

If a rationally organized novel or translation can thus be read as a representation and instantiation of "sanity" produced through what Michel Foucault calls "discipline," an experimental novel like *Finnegans Wake* or an experimental translation such as I am here modeling on the *Wake* can plausibly be read as a representation and instantiation of "insanity"—psychosis—emerging out of the breakdown of societal discipline.

Given that Lacan's lectures on Joyce (the twenty-third seminar, titled *The Sinthome* [2016]) are manifestly a representation and instantiation of Lacan's proudly touted discourse of the hysteric, it should go without saying that he is not repressively advocating a restoration of

6 In *Translating the Perception of Text* (2012b) Clive Scott seems to hint at something like this displaced djreamish "realism," which he specifically (and persuasively) aligns with surrealism (90):

> Translation is the act by which we reveal to ourselves, and to other readers, what a text has made available to us in terms of linguistic experience and the renewal of perceptual consciousness. Clearly, this experience and renewal of consciousness are not evident in the source text, since it is only through the reader that they come into being: in translating the source text, the reader is translating his/her readerly experience into existence. (xi)

We return to take a closer look at Scott on translating-as-overwriting in section 2o.

rationalist discipline; rather, as we'll see toward the end of Chapter 2, he is insisting that we read late Joyce as an *engagement* with psychosis that also *courts* psychosis.

And this book explicitly extends that insistence to experimental translation as well—though I suppose I would shift the emphasis slightly, from "engaging psychosis" to "engaging the rationalist discipline that masters psychosis, by deviating from it in playful ways."

1z

Let me close this Preface with a discussion forum post from one of my MA students at the Chinese University of Hong Kong, Shenzhen, in spring semester, 2023:

> As someone who's dabbled in experimental translation myself, I can say that it's both thrilling and challenging. One of my favorite experiments was taking a short story and translating it into a poem, using free association and imagery to capture the essence of the original work. It was a bit of a risk, as poetry and prose are very different forms of expression, but in the end, it created a totally unique and powerful piece of writing.
>
> Another time, I experimented with found poetry, taking fragments of text from various sources and piecing them together to create a new work. It was a bit like a puzzle, trying to find the right words and phrases to fit together in a way that made sense and conveyed meaning. But in the end, it was a rewarding experience, as the final product was something that I never would have created using traditional translation methods.
>
> Of course, not every experiment is going to be a success. I've had plenty of failed attempts and false starts, where my ideas just didn't quite come together in the way I had hoped. But that's all part of the process—experimentation is about taking risks and trying new things, even if they don't always work out.
>
> Overall, my experiences with experimental translation have taught me that there's so much more to language and communication than just the words on the page. By breaking free from traditional boundaries and exploring new approaches to translation, we can create works of art that challenge, inspire, and engage readers in new and unexpected ways.
>
> LIANG Siting, Stella (May 6, 2023)

2 Translouting into Djreamish

Finnegans Wake, then, as a translation—or a "translouting"—of the 1864 street ballad "Finigan's Wake" (or some other imagined source text) into an invented djream language: an obvious place to start.

If this book explores lessons experimental translators can learn from *Finnegans Wake*, surely the first lesson (Chapter 2) should be tied to how Joyce himself *translated.*

Later lessons can be structured more loosely around analogies between how Joyce *wrote* (without necessarily translating—Chapter 3) and how the experimental translator inspired by Joyce might *write* a translation (Chapter 4).

2a

As it happens, Fritz Senn, "the foremost practitioner of Joycean translation studies" (O'Neill 2005: 12[1]), can help us get started, in an article

1 See O'Neill (2005) for a recurring (and admiring, though critical) engagement with Senn's account of Joyce on translation, dealing with *Finnegans Wake* on pages 27, 35, 58, 59, 61, 126, and with translation on 8, 56, 230n9, 242nll.

O'Neill is apparently too modest to say that Senn is the foremost scholar of *Joyce translating* and that he himself is the foremost scholar of *translating Joyce*: see O'Neill (2005, 2013, 2022).

True, Senn has also engaged German translations of the *Wake*—see e.g. Senn (1970, 1978, 1993, 1998)—but with none of the breadth of O'Neill's scholarship, dealing with partial or complete translations of the *Wake* into 26 languages (not to mention the poststructuralist complexity of his theorization of translation, for which see Chapter 5).

Surprisingly, however, even in his most recent book, *Finnegans Wakes: Tales of Translation*, O'Neill (2022) does not cite Senn (2013).

DOI: 10.4324/9781003470427-2

titled "How Joyce Translates Himself" (2013). Senn covers all four of Joyce's books: *Dubliners* on one page (124), *A Portrait of the Artist as a Young Man* on a page and a half (125–26), *Ulysses* on nearly six pages (126–32), and *Finnegans Wake* on the remaining four and a half pages (132–36). But let's stick with the *Wake*.[2]

He begins by noting that the book's title is itself already a translation, from the ballad's title (with an apostrophe), which he writes as *Finnegan's Wake*, to *Finnegans Wake*. The ballad was originally printed in 1864 with the title "Finigan's Wake"; scholars have frequently assimilated the "Finigan" spelling to the "correct" Irish "Finnegan," but that is itself a translation; and since the original ballad was published on three pages, jumping from the standard quotation marks ("Finigan's Wake") to the italics reserved for books (*Finnegan's Wake*) is another.

Senn notes that embedded in Joyce's title are three foreign words: French *fin* "end," Latin *negans* "negating," and German *Gans* "goose." The first two are thematically suggestive—they seem usefully to predict the endlessness of the tale Joyce tells—but the "significance, or validity, if any" of the third "does not seem to have been shown" (132).

And he comments: "Such stray semantemes, tangential possibilities, are an intrinsic hazard of the lexical wide sweep" (132).

So what do we do with that last, the *ganz* (German for "completely") irrelevant "tangential possibility" of German *Gans* "goose"?

Do we simply ignore it? Do we adopt a more activist stance and firmly banish it as the uninvited and unmotivated invention of the overingenious critic?

Should we assume that Joyce *intended* for us to spot the negation of an ending in *fin-negans* and had no interest in linking the German goose to his title and book?

More sanctimoniously: should we build the implied warning or disclaimer of "Such stray semantemes, tangential possibilities, are an intrinsic hazard of the lexical wide sweep" into a moral condemnation of experimental translation?

"Once graphic units are broken up," Senn adds, "there is no obvious limit. Common sense or consensus rarely helps" (132).

2 Your moment of Senn: "Joyce tends to go to extremes – and beyond them, as in *Finnegans Wake*" (2013: 123).

So perhaps we should not break up graphic units at all? Perhaps the whole premise of this chapter as a lesson for experimental translators, and indeed of the book as a whole, should be dismissed as gaslighting, to be dispelled (or at least goosed) by "common sense or consensus"?

2b

Obviously the fact that I continue writing past that last question implies a decisive *no* answer, or perhaps my sense that the question was "purely" (as if anything were ever "purely" anything) rhetorical.

But I think it's worth bearing dismissive commonsensical reactions to experiments like this in mind, not only as preparation for external attacks but as an internalized tension.

Experimental translation, like all experimental work, is *predicated* on that tension.

There is always, must always be, or perhaps just always tends to be, an inclination to reject the experiment out of hand—and an exploratory resistance to that inclination.

2c

Senn next explores some numerical translations, of threes into Roman III or Arabic 111 "one hundred eleven," and those into Kiswahili, Hebrew, and other languages, and lists of multilingual translations of individual words "often of twenty-nine items, the number of days in February[—at least in Leap Year—]relating a lunar cycle" (133).

He gives one example of what he notes are the "numerous phrases accept[ing] readings in different languages," namely "Warum night!" (479.36), which as he notes "is equidistant from English *Warm night* and German *Warum nicht?* 'why not?'; in each case there is one aberrant or missing letter" (133).

There are of course many similar cases in the *Wake*; one that is better known to translation scholars, because Jacques Derrida dwells on it as untranslatable in "Des tours de Babel" (1985: 214–15 in French, 170–71 in English), is "And he war": "And shall not Babel be with Lebab? And he war. And he shall open his mouth and answer on which: I hear, O Ismael, how they laud is only as my loud is one" (258.11-13).

War is not only an armed conflict in English but the German for "was," the past tense of "to be." The "one aberrant or missing letter" in this latter case is limited to that word "war": the implicit German sentence behind the English would be "und er war" (and he was).

Go ahead, Teague (or Thady): translaud "how they laud is only as my loud is one" out loud into djreamish.

2d

Most of the rest of Senn's examples are homophonic translations (or what the Outranspo calls "sonotranslations" [see Robert-Foley 2020, 2023]), or what Joyce might want to call *translautings*, or *Überlautungen*, translations of the sounds of individual syllables. In the *Wake* some are sonotranslated directly from a foreign language, others through an intermediate language. (Senn isn't aware of this translation-studies nomenclature: he calls them English "approximations," "refractions," and "mutations" of foreign sentences.)

His first example is one that immediately follows "Warum night?" in *Finnegans Wake*, namely "Conning two lay payees" (*FW* 479.36-480.1) as a homophonic translation of French *Connais-tu le pays?* ("Do you know the country?").

He follows that up immediately with a series of homophonic translations that seem unrelated in English because each sonotranslates/translauts an idiomatic translation into a different language of "How do you do today, my light (or dark) sir?":

> "Come on, fool porterfull, hosiered women blown monk sewer?" (from French: *Comment vous portez-vous aujourd'hui, mon blanc monsieur?* ["How are you (carrying yourself), my white sir?"]; *FW* 16.4; Senn omits "aujourd'hui")
>
> "Huru more Nee, minny frickans?" (from Swedish: *Hur mår ni, mina fröken?* ["How are you, my misses?"]; *FW* 54.10)
>
> "Comb his tar odd gee sing your mower O meeow?" (through Italian: *Come sta oggi, signor moro mio?* ["How are you today, my dark/Moorish sir?"]; *FW* 409.14)
>
> "Fee gate has Heenan hoity, mind uncle Hare?" (from German: *Wie geht es Ihnen heute, mein dunkler Herr?* ["How goes it with you today, my dark sir?"]; *FW* 466.29)

Those are just the four that Senn gives (134); as he notes, the *Wake* has "over a dozen other incarnations" of that homophonic translation history. Here is one other:

"Guinness thaw tool in jew me dinner ouzel fin?" (from Irish: *Conas tá tú indiu mo dhuine uasal fionn?* ["How are you today my fair gentleman?"]; *FW* 35.15-16)[3]

2e

A quick insert: Alexander Ullman (2018) has an article titled "The Sound of Translation: Joyce, the Zukofskys, and Liturgical *Piyutim*," supposedly beginning with a reading of translation in the *Wake*—but Ullman never really engages with translation in Joyce's novel.[4]

3 Jacques Lacan takes a shot at these Joycean self-translautings as well, in "Joyce the Symptom":

> The most extreme case, I can tell you, and I owe this to Jacques Aubert, is— *Who ails tongue coddeau, aspace of dumbillsilly?* [*FW* 15.18] Had I come across this piece of writing on my own, would I have perceived or not— *Où est ton cadeau, espèce d'imbecile?* Where's your present, you imbecile?
>
> What is unprecedented in this is that the homophony, translinguistic homophony on this occasion, is sustained only by letters that conform to English-language spelling. You wouldn't know that *who* is pronounced that way in the interrogative. There is some kind of ambiguity in this phonetic usage, which I would also spell *f.a.u.n.* The faunesque aspect of the thing leans squarely upon the letter, namely upon something that is not essential to a tongue, a tongue being something woven by the accidents of history.
>
> Price 2016: 145

4 Ullman's opening line does not inspire confidence:

> In the 2012 third edition of the *Translation Studies Reader*, translator and scholar Lawrence Venuti situates the history of Western translation theory and practice—from its inception in the Roman translation of the Hebrew Bible through John Dryden's translation of Homer to Google Translate—as divided between two different discursive strategies: the word-for-word strategy and the sense-for-sense strategy.
>
> Ullman 2018: 43

First off, who doesn't know that thinking about translation has traditionally been focused on the distinction between word-for-word and sense-for-sense translation? Do we really need Venuti's introductions to the *Translation Studies Reader* to learn this?

But second, not even Venuti claims that "Western translation theory and practice" begins in "the Roman translation of the Hebrew Bible." He says that it begins not in Herodotus, nor in reports and discussions of the *Greek* translation of the Hebrew Bible, which for me in *Western Translation Theory from Herodotus to Nietzsche*

(He does engage with translation in the Zukofskys' *Catullus* and the *Piyutim.*) He doesn't cite Senn (2013), which as we've seen does explore Joyce's self-translations in the *Wake*.

His dismissive summation of "translation between two languages" in the *Wake* is that it "is narrated … by smashing words into each other or by carrying a biblical text into a new language" (51).

That biblical text that he says Joyce "carr[ies] into a new language" is Genesis 11, the "translation" chapter on the Tower of Babel. What Ullman calls the "carrying [of] a biblical text," however, is a very (roama)loose retelling and thus a "translation" only in the experimental sense in which "Since the bouts of Hebear and Hairyman the cornflowers have been staying at Ballymun" (section 1t) is a translation of Quinet's "*Aujourd'hui comme aux temps de Pline et de Columelle la jacinthe se plaît dans les Gaules, la pervenche en Illyrie*":

> Oftwhile balbulous, mithre ahead, with goodly trowel in grasp and ivoroiled overalls which he habitacularly fondseed, like Haroun Childeric Eggeberth he would caligulate by multiplicables the alltitude and malltitude until he seesaw by neatlight of the

(1997/2014: 4-6) is the *second* stage in the development of Western translation theory and practice, but in Cicero's *De optimo genere oratorum* ("On the Best Kind of Orators") in 46 BCE (2012: 13).

It is certainly true, however, that Cicero's treatise launches the opposition between translating word for word and translating sense for sense. I start the clock earlier because I don't restrict "Western translation theory and practice" to that psychomachy between word and sense.

Venuti does refer to Jerome's Latin Vulgate translation and recognition that "the Gospels … contain various free renderings of the Hebrew Bible that differ from the Septuagint" (15)—and Jerome recognizes this in Latin, the language of the Roman Empire. But Jerome himself was an Illyrian, not a Roman.

But even if we think of Jerome's Vulgate Old Testament as a "Roman translation of the Hebrew Scriptures," (a) he also translated the New Testament from Greek, and (b) he did so in the late fourth century BCE, nearly half a millennium after Cicero first began to theorize sense-for-sense translation and more than six centuries after the Greek (Septuagint) translation of the Hebrew Scriptures (which is what Ullman seems to be referring to, all unawares).

One final note: Venuti neither anthologizes nor cites Dryden's translation of Homer. On p. 39, in the excerpt he anthologizes from Dryden's *Preface to Ovid's Epistles*, he gives us Dryden's brief Greek quotation from the second line of the *Odyssey*, and on p. 42 he gives us Robert Fagles' 1996 English translation of that passage. Venuti gives us no hint that Dryden ever translated Homer.

> liquor wheretwin 'twas born, his roundhead staple of other days to rise in undress maisonry upstanded (joygrantit!), a waalworth of a skyerscape of most eyeful hoyth entowerly, erigenating from next to nothing and celescalating the himals and all, hierarchitectitiptitoploftical, with a burning bush abob off its baubletop and with larrons o'toolers clittering up and tombles a'buckets clottering down.
>
> *FW* 4.30-5.4

Is this a translation? Ullman demurs, saying that Joyce too "suspends the question":

> But is this a word-for-word translation or a sense-for-sense translation of Genesis 11? Joyce suspends the question by an emphasis on sound. If read aloud, the performance of this excerpt always limits its textual reach: one has to make certain choices, at once liberating the sound from its textual apparatus and also limiting its polyphony. Translation occurs here across various levels: between Genesis 11 and the text, between the text on the page and the voice of the reader, and between the voice of the reader and the ear of the listener. The scene foregrounds sound as a necessary medium of translation, one that implicates the reader and the listener in its process of moving across these various points of origin and destination.
>
> Ullman 2018: 47

I would say instead that Joyce *transforms* the question, by radically expanding the technical scope of translating via the experimental techniques that I explore and deploy in this book.

2f

The narrow and rather crabbed sense in which "Joyce suspends the question [of translation] by an emphasis on sound" would appear to be the traditional understanding of translation as the disembodied reproduction of sentential semantics. Since "translauting" the sounds of the source text's syllables precludes semantic equivalence, presumably, interlingual homophony "suspends the question of translation."

But then Ullman also wants to explore "sound as a necessary medium of translation." On the one hand, the emphasis on sound (and not sense) suspends the question of translation; on the other, in Joyce sound becomes "a necessary medium of translation." The radical sonification of translation completely vacates semantics and thus suspends translation. Sonotranslation somehow remains translation but also suspends the question of translation.

This is what happens when one studies experimental translation without a theoretical or practical grasp of experimental translation. Nothing makes sense. Radical departures from hegemonic forms and structures remain enshrouded in fog, and get treated as middles to be (sort of vaguely) excluded.

Ullman seems to unpack that sonic "necessary medium of translation" in lines like "Joyce creates a network of sounds not simply thematically or homophonically but also at the level of the puns of the word 'babel'"—but how exactly does this signify translation that is "not just thematic or homophonic" but "the creation of a network of sounds"?

What is that "network," and how is creating one different from what every brilliant writer does?

I'm here to argue that the difference lies in several specific techniques of experimental translation. Ullman seems to hint in that direction with "not simply thematically or homophonically," but his hints remain not only vague and unexplored but semi-negated. "Not just homophonically" suggests that Joyce is also translating homophonically, but that that is a secondary or peripheral technique that can be set aside in favor of "the creation of a network of sounds." But even that suggestion is only implied—left for the reader to guess at.

And here: "The phrases at times have an aquatic valence—not literal translations but 'littoral' ones" (48).

What is a "littoral" translation? Lily Robert-Foley (2023) devotes almost her entire third chapter to that sound-pun, drawing and commenting on Noel (2021), who draws and comments on Glissant (1981; Dash 1992 in English).

Ullman in 2018 could not have known Noel (2021) or Robert-Foley (2023), of course, but he gives no sign that he is aware of Glissant (1981) either, which in 2018 had been around for 37 years in French, or Dash (1992), which for 26 years would have saved him the trouble of translating from Glissant's French.

Without that kind of help, "littoral translation" remains a clever but nebulous pun for him—but then the middle he excludes between "translation as the accurate production of disembodied semantics" and "sonic (non)translation" leads him to read Joyce's punning portmanteaux in the *Wake* as completely lacking in meaning, so that there is no point trying to understand, theorize, or translate anything: "But to derive any meaning from any reference is to separate the words from a plot that is itself almost completely composed of puns and portmanteau words, thus offering no definitive way to translate or make sense of the babble (Attridge [1988]: 149)" (48).

"No definitive way to translate": is there ever a *definitive* way?[5]

5 It is telling that Ullman relies on Attridge's Chomskyan objectification of puns as structurally located on a continuum "from the totally powerless item, devoid of meaning because already completely specified by its surroundings, to the infinitely powerful item, devoid of meaning because completely unspecified":

> The context will now allow only one meaning to be perceived in the gap which it occupies, and anything—or nothing at all—will be interpreted as providing that meaning. In the terms used by information theory, the more predictable a given item in a message, the less information it carries; the totally predictable word conveys, in itself, absolutely nothing. What we have, then, is a continuum from the totally powerless item, devoid of meaning because already completely specified by its surroundings, to the infinitely powerful item, devoid of meaning because completely unspecified. Meaning resides between the two. What we call the pun is one stage along the way; what we call "single meaning" is another. Exclude the pun, and you exclude the process on which all language rests: the process whereby context constrains but does not wholly constrain the possibilities of meaning (142).

Information theory of course, like Chomsky's TG-grammar, radically dehumanizes human perception and interpretation (see also Sun 2023 for discussion). "Colorless green ideas sleep furiously" *just is* meaningless, for Chomsky; "the totally predictable word *just does* convey[], in itself, absolutely nothing," for Attridge. There's nothing a poet or the reader of a poem can do with those colorless green ideas or that totally predictable word. *Nothing*. Human beings are completely powerless in the face of the alien objectivity of language. It's not that human beings impose meanings on language, but that "contexts" "allow" meanings. It's not that human beings interpret; this or that structure "*will be interpreted* as providing that meaning." Interpretation is a dehumanized event depicted in the passive voice, with no agent. As Ullman puts it, *Finnegans Wake* is "almost completely composed of puns and portmanteau words, thus offering no definitive way to translate or make sense of the babble": the structural context has to *offer* a definite way to translate or make sense, and since for Ullman the *Wake* makes no such offer, there is absolutely no way for us to understand or translate it. Human beings have no interpretive workarounds that enable us to make sense of apparent nonsense, or to translate the apparently untranslatable. Our hands are tied.

I read this linguistic objectivism as a deep-seated slave morality that works unconsciously to protect the source text against ("mis")reading and (experimental "mis-")

The "babble" seems to refer to the *Wake*; the impulse to translate would seem to be felt by speakers of other languages, and Ullman seems to condemn them to failure due to the lack of a "definitive" way to "make sense of the babble."

"Fluid transfer" in "In repeatedly inverting babel, Joyce initiates a fluid transfer between voices, languages, geographies, and identities while also resuscitating stories that the modern state seeks to leave out" (48) also seems to hint metaphorically at translation (are we talking about hydraulics? canalization?) without actually engaging it.

As for "smashing words into each other"—surely Joyce's construction of the "target language" that I'm calling "djreamish" out of invented portmanteau words is a little more complicated than that? (See section 2j for a closer look.)

Reading Fritz Senn (2013) might have helped him.

2g

So what can the experimental translator do with a homophonic series like the one Senn traces? Homophonic translation is perhaps the most-practiced and best-known experimental strategy in translation; Ullman's discussion of the Zukofskys' *Catullus* (1969) reminds us of that, but there are of course many others, including van Rooten (1967) and David Melnick (1983, 2015). (See Robinson 2023b: 100–4 for discussion.)

What Joyce's series of homophonic translations through intermediate languages seems to suggest is that a shortish text—a poem or a short story, or even an essay—might be translated experimentally using this serial shift: every line or stanza or paragraph translated homophonically through a different intermediate language.

translation. If the source text *controls* our ability to read and understand it, then the only thing a translator can do with a properly rational source text is to translate it properly, rationally, which is to say subserviently. The problem with *Finnegans Wake* for Ullman is that it is not properly rational, and that makes (proper) translation impossible.

Lessons Experimental Translators Can Learn from Finnegans Wake is organized around a radical rejection of every carceral tenet in that slave morality.

2h

For example: section 4a of this book, the first section of "Benjamins Totin' Vodka."

My first experimental translation of Walter Benjamin's "Aufgabe des Übersetzers" (as "Th' Upgiving o' th' O'ersetter," 2023a) used a slightly modified version of the experimental translation strategy that Benjamin himself championed, the etymological literalism of Friedrich Hölderlin's translations of Pindar and Sophocles.

But once that translation had whetted my appetite for experimental forays out beyond sense-for-sense approaches to translating Benjamin—the strategy that he attacked and all of his previous English translators have followed—I conceived the idea of showcasing a variety of experimental strategies, a different one in each of Benjamin's eleven paragraphs.

My strategy for the first (and the title) was a homophonic rendering directly from Benjamin's German:

> **Die Aufgabe des Übersetzers**
>
> Nirgends erweist sich einem Kunstwerk oder einer Kunstform gegenüber die Rücksicht auf den Aufnehmenden für deren Erkenntnis fruchtbar. Nicht genug, daß jede Beziehung auf ein bestimmtes Publikum oder dessen Repräsentanten vom Wege abführt, ist sogar der Begriff eines ›idealen‹ Aufnehmenden in allen kunsttheoretischen Erörterungen vom Übel, weil diese lediglich gehalten sind, Dasein und Wesen des Menschen überhaupt vorauszusetzen. So setzt auch die Kunst selbst dessen leibliches und geistiges Wesen voraus — seine Aufmerksamkeit aber in keinem ihrer Werke. Denn kein Gedicht gilt dem Leser, kein Bild dem Beschauer, keine Symphonie der Hörerschaft.
>
> Benjamin 1923/1972: 9

> **D'oof-gobble Dusk Over Seltzers**
>
> Near guns airviced sick eyenumb coonswork odor ionair coonsform gaygunuber d'rucksicked off deign oofneighmendin' fir Derringer Kentness freakedbar. Nicked canoed doss yay-duh Betsy hung aw fine beigetimidness booblickem odor dressin' reppraisin' tauntin' foam vague upfirth; its cigar dare bagrift eyeness

> "e-day-all-in" oofneighmendin' in Holland cooinstareawaytishin' aireartherrungin' foamable, vile diesel ladygleek gayhalten sinned, dawesine and vazin' dusk mention overhopped for owlzoosensin'. So sets ouch dicundus cellbust dissin' loblickess und geisty guess vazin' for owls—zany owlsmixemkite auburn in kinda mere or fairkey. Den kine gaydicked guilt dame laser, kine build dame bayshower, gynesymphony dare whorrorshaft.
>
> Robinson 2024b

I could of course have continued in that same vein, sonotranslating all 194 of Benjamin's German sentences into this kind of fractured English; but that seemed like a recipe for the target reader's tedium. So as I say, I tried out a new experimental strategy in every paragraph, except the third, where I used one method (serial DeepL translation) on the first sentence, "Übersetzung ist eine Form" ("translation is a form"), and ended up 19 languages later back at German with "Die Übersetzungen werden in den folgenden Formaten erstellt" ("The translations will be constructed/created in the following formats")—and then translated the rest of that paragraph literally from Benjamin's German.

A later paragraph, Paragraph 9, uses a strategy similar to Joyce's serial homophonic translations, but serial literalism instead of sonotranslation—namely, what the Outranspo calls "grammatically extended neotranslation," a literal translation from an intermediate translation, in this case specifically a literal translation of Leevi Lehto's Finnish translation of Benjamin's essay, "Kääntäjän tehtävä" (1991/2007: 46–49).

2i

But what now if we were to apply Joyce's serial translautory strategy to Benjamin's essay, a translauting of each paragraph not from the German but from a series of translations of the essay into different languages?

To illustrate that strategy, I started translauting whole paragraphs of Benjamin's essay, following that rendition from Benjamin's first paragraph above with homophonic translations from French, Russian, Spanish, Chinese, and Finnish translations—but then decided to mix that strategy in with the other ones I explore in this book, especially the building of portmanteau words (starting in the next section) and the use of heteronyms (Chapter 3), and print the whole thing as Chapter 4.

2j

The experimental writing style for which the *Wake* is famous is not, of course, homophonic translation but the insistent blending (or for Ullman "smashing") of sixty-odd languages into portmanteau words.

For example, from the novel's opening page:

> Sir Tristram, violer d'amores, fr'over the short sea, had passencore rearrived from North Armorica on this side the scraggy isthmus of Europe Minor to wielderfight his penisolate war: nor had topsawyer's rocks by the stream Oconee exaggerated themselse to Laurens County's gorgios while they went doublin their mumper all the time: nor avoice from afire bellowsed mishe mishe to tauftauf thuartpeatrick: not yet, though venissoon after, had a kidscad buttended a bland old Isaac …
>
> *FW* 3.4-11

Sir Tristram or Tristan is the hero of the medieval romance who was tragically in love with Isolde of Ireland, and the daughter in the *Wake* is (djream-)named Isolde, or Issy for short; but there are other possible Sir Tristrams as well, such as Sir Amory Tristram, the Norman conqueror of the Danes (in 1177) who ruled Ireland. Joyce's incorporation of his given name Amory in "violer d'amores," (English) violist/(French) violate of loves/Amorys, gives us the first portmanteau in the passage.

The second is "passencore." It hints at two French phrases, *pas encore* ("not yet") and *passe encore* ("not bad"), but also Latin *cor* ("heart"); Joyce wrote to Harriet Shaw Weaver that it was also intended to hint at the "ricorsi storici of Vico," the endless returns or recursions (and in this paragraph "rearrivals") around which he spun the various tales that make up the *Wake*.

The third is "wielderfight," which builds German *wieder* "again" and Dutch *wiel* "wheel" into "wielder" (someone who wields power or uses something skillfully) and that plus "fight' into a hint at German *wiederfechten* (refight).

The fourth is "penisolate," referring to Sir Arthur Wellesley's British forces invading Portugal in August, 1808, to fight a "peninsular war"; but it also has "penis" and "isolate" built into it.

"Topsawyer's rocks by the stream Oconee exaggerated themselse to Laurens County's gorgios while they went doublin" is complicated: "doublin" refers to Joyce's Dublin, obviously, but also to Dublin, Georgia, a town in Laurens County on the Oconee River, founded by a Dubliner named Jonathan Sawyer. *Gorgios* is a Roma term for non-Roma, but also hints at Georgia; a topsawyer is a sawpit worker who stands on a high platform above the timber, but there is also a Topsawyer's Rock on the Oconee near Dublin, and Sawyer of course refers to the Irish founder of the town as well.

In Irish "mishe" is "I am," and Joyce explained to Harriet Shaw Weaver that the implied continuation is "a Christian"; but it also hints at Moshe, the Hebrew for the prophetic stutterer we call Moses, who, when God called to him from the burning bush (Exodus 3:2), said "He-he-here I am." A "mish" in Serbian (and other Slavic languages) is a mouse, which hints at Maurice Behan, who figures in a story that Joyce retold from the *Freeman's Journal* of November 21, 1923. Behan was a store caretaker who reported being awakened from sleep by two men trying to break in. Roy Benjamin (2013: 672), drawing on both Ellmann's biography (1959/1982: 546–47) and Bill Cadbury's (2007: 73) "genetic guide" to chapters 1.2-4, notes that Joyce was referencing Freud's claim that external noises heard while dreaming are built into the dream—what Roy Benjamin calls "the most intimate and solipsistic example of coding meaningless noise into meaningful pattern":

> As the *Wake* translates the story, "This battering babel allower the door …was not in the very remotest like the belzey babble of a bottle of boose which would not rouse him out o' slumber deep" (64.9–12). The reference to the tower of Babel suggests the transformation of a single master code ("the whole earth had one language") into a cacophony of competing codes, as God confuses "the language of all the earth" (Gen 11.1.9). The biblical conflation of "babel" (meaning "gate of god") with the Hebrew word "balal," meaning "confuse," further emphasizes the degeneration of divine code into incomprehensible noise. The collective enterprise of building a tower to the heavens ends in the scattering of monadic individuals over the earth.
>
> Benjamin 2013: 672

"Taufen" is German for "to baptize" and "to name"; "thouartpeatrick" baptizes and names someone "Patrick" but also "Peter," from the New Testament story of Jesus saying "Thou art Peter [*petros*] and upon this rock [*petra*] I will build my church" (Matthew 16:18, *KJV*).

"Venissoon" is obviously "venison" but also "very soon"; the story here is of "bland old Isaac" (blind old Isaac) letting his younger son ("kidscad" = "kid cadet" + the "kidskin" Jacob uses to disguise himself) the venison-purveyor Jacob steal his older son Esau's birthright with the butt end of a gun (Genesis 25-35, where of course there is no gun).

Some general observations, then: Joyce's portmanteau words enable the morphological and syntactic layering of story, of history and myth, of human weakness and virtue, into every sentence in the 600-page novel. The resulting language, which Clive Hart calls "Djoytsch" and Joyce (in a sense) called "turfish" (and I'm calling "djreamish"), is difficult to read with "waking" (fully conscious) understanding of all those layers; it is djreamlike mainly in its radical distortions of idiomatic English.

The narrative is djreamlike in other ways as well, most notably that the narrator is asleep and is only *projecting* the various characters and events; we'll explore that heteronymous djreaminess more fully in Chapter 3.

2k

What now about translouting into portmanteau djreamish?

Let's start here: one of the oldest memes about translation is that it is lossy—that there are always aspects of the source text that can't be translated, or that a single translation can never capture everything in the source text. Three or four or five translations of the same work might come close, if each privileged a different aspect.

"Lost in translation," then, would be a defining *irrationality* of translation. It would entail our normative "unconscious" tendency to focus on one specific aspect of a source text, especially the semantic meanings of sentences as idiomatically rendered in the target language, and ignore the rest as irrelevant.

All that would be a bad dream—but a bad dream dolled up as empirical reality.

What we typically do with that irrationality, of course, that naturalized bad dream, is to ignore it. Pretend it doesn't exist. Get on with the translating. No point thinking about implausibilities when there is work to be done, money to be earned.

2l

What translation scholars of a certain stripe do instead with that irrationality is to systematize it—remaster it as a more complex rationality.

The standard way to rationalize the irrational lossiness of translation has been text-type theory: when translating an *informative* text we organize the translation around the accurate reproduction of the information and let the prosodics and other stylistic features be lost; when translating an *expressive* text we organize the translation around the effective reproduction of expressive style and let strict semantic equivalence be lost; when translating an *operative* text we organize the translation around the effective reproduction of the persuasive speech act, and so on.

That way the "loss" of expressivity and operativity in translating an informative text is not really a loss at all, because expressivity and operativity are not really relevant to the text type.

And so on for the other two as well. Problem solved! (This framework is from Katharina Reiß 1981.)

2m

This kind of Enlightenment rationality seems increasingly insecure and obsessive in the age of Freud and Lacan, Derrida and Deleuze—and James Joyce.

Are we so afraid of the dark that we have to keep the lights on in our laboratories to facilitate the building of ever more elaborate engines of self-protection?

2n

One ambition an ambitious experimental translouter might conceive on this head would be to translate *everything*—the whole source text.

Not to settle for half-measures; not to impose nervous hierarchies on the task, this because it's important but not that because it's irrelevant; to translout *all* of that gaswind into turfish, or djreamish.

Translouting as an overt exploration of the bad faith lurking just behind the disguising of that bad normative dream as empirical reality. That exploration dolled up as a *good* dream.

But how?

20

In *Translating the Perception of Text* Clive Scott (2012b: 62) advocates what he calls "overwriting" as "the inescapable 'textual condition' of a translation which seeks to do justice to the phenomenology of reading and to the Merleau-Pontian invisibility of the source text":

> This textual condition is the condition of being overwritten, either quite literally, as a layering of palimpsestic superimpositions, or as an ungovernable multiplication or series of texts. The reasons for this inexorable growth of text, the growth towards actual or virtual illegibility (understood literally and/or metaphorically), are, roughly speaking, twofold: the reincarnation of translation as translationwork entails an endless process of inclusive modulation; and part of that inclusiveness is the text's incorporation of the multi-sensory, or the text's implication or supposition of the multi-sensory.
>
> Scott 2012b: 62

That "inexorable growth of text, the growth towards actual or virtual illegibility," is for Scott a "multi-perspectivalism" that "does not lead to a distillation, to a *synthetic* portrait of the landscape; it leads to an unruly hold-all of the manifold" (see also Scott 2012a and 2018). Or, as Joyce would put it in the *Wake*, it leads to a "crossmess parzel" (619.5). And Scott's account of the reader phenomenology that seems to inspire this kind of crossmessy translation does sound remarkably like the *Wake*:

> The more we look at or read something, the more its dimensions multiply. We imagine this condition as the source of Cézanne's "obsessive" mode of looking. Our own pursuit of the multilingual translation is, we might say, the attempt to rid translation of monocular perspectivalism. We have already had much to say about translation's effort to reveal the invisible, which is contained in, and the condition of, visibility. Invisibility we understand as that latent multi-perspectivalism that we can never properly achieve, that we can only point to. But we must always be on the move towards it.
>
> Scott 2012b: 62

2p

Where Scott deviates from Joyce, obviously, is in the specific multi-perspectivalizing strategy/-ies he chooses: where Joyce rebuilds the English language at the morphological level, word-bit by word-bit, and syntactically, phrase-bit by phrase-bit, Scott argues for creating multiple translations and printing them on top of each other, as in Figure 2.1.

Ainsi (2), toujours poussés (4) vers de nouveaux (4) rivages (2),

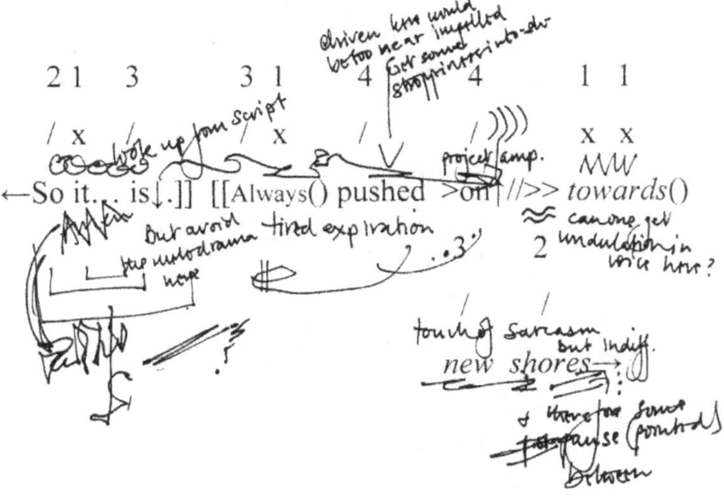

[ ] = resistance between units; ( ) = impulse to speak, to choose a word; >> = pressure to drive on; italics = accelerando; reduction to 16-point = slight recession of voice; ↑↓ = pitch rise/fall; ←→ = continuing voice at level pitch

Figure 2.1 "Translation of the first line of Lamartine's 'Le Lac', with over-writing and doodling" (Scott 2012b: 69).

Figure 2.1 is actually quite readable; it resembles a lot of second drafts of original source texts from the time before computers. In touting "the growth towards actual or virtual illegibility," however, Scott seems to hint that Figure 2.1's relative high legibility illustrates an early stage of that growth. Figure 2.2 perhaps reflects a later stage.

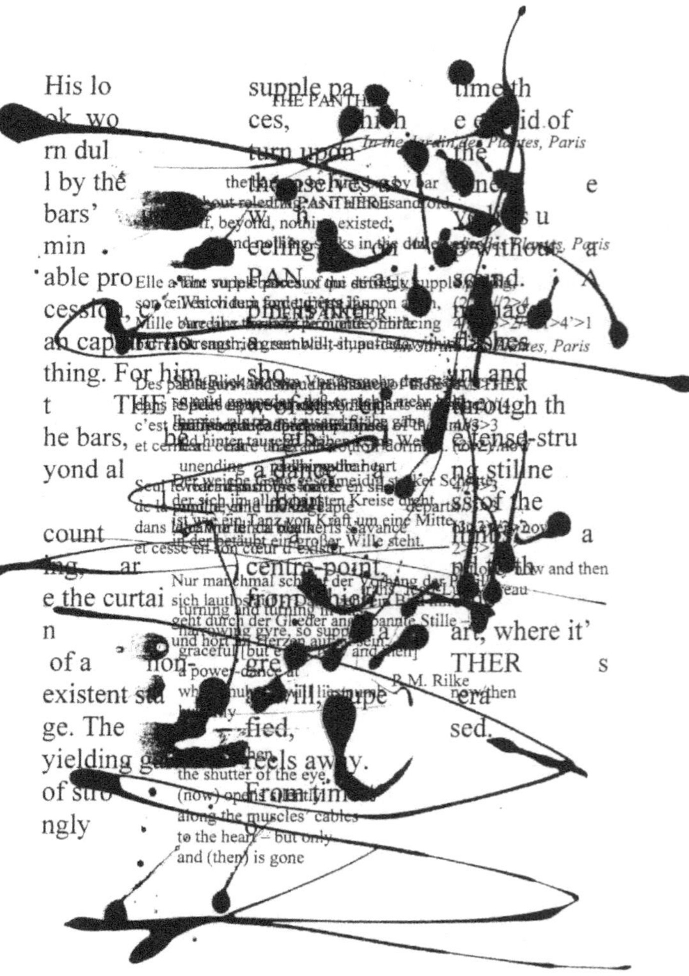

Figure 2.2 "Overprinted translation of Rilke's 'Der Panther', with ink doodling" (Scott 2012b: 79).

That is obviously illegible in a way very different from Joyce's *Wake*. If Scott calls for translations to be "overwritten, either quite literally, as a layering of palimpsestic superimpositions, or as an ungovernable multiplication or series of texts," Joyce does both, in a way.

We have seen the "ungovernable multiplication or series of texts" in connection with Joyce's serial transloutings of the Edgar Quinet gaswind into turfish in sections 1q-u and 2e and serial homophonic translautings in section 2d; through his multilingual portmanteau words now he arguably overwrites his drafts as a *metaphorical* "layering of palimpsestic superimpositions."

How then might we move Scott's literal layering of the "unruly hold-all of the manifold" more closely into alignment with Joyce's metaphorical layering of that manifold?

2q

In *Critical Translation Studies* (Robinson 2017b: 41–51) I noted a confusion in Lydia Liu's (1999) reading of Marx's translational analogy in the *Grundrisse*. That confusion stemmed from a misleading English translation by Martin Nicolaus (bracketed letters added to both paragraphs):

> [a] Die Ideen existieren nicht getrennt von der Sprache. Ideen, die aus ihrer Muttersprache erst in eine fremde Sprache übersetzt werden müssen, um zu kursieren, um austauschbar zu werden, bieten schon mehr Analogie; die Analogie liegt dann aber nicht in [b] der Sprache, sondern in [c] ihrer Fremdheit.
>
> Marx 1939: n.p.

> [a] Ideas do not exist separately from language. Ideas which have first to be translated out of their mother tongue into a foreign tongue in order to circulate, in order to become exchangeable, offer a somewhat better analogy; but the analogy then lies not in [b] the language, but in the foreign quality [*Fremdheit*] of [c] language.
>
> Nicolaus 1973: 21–22, as quoted with the bracketed insertion of *Fremdheit* by Shell 1982: 106

The source of the problem is the syntactic difference between *die Sprache* in German and "(the) language" in English: because

Germans never say just plain *Sprache*, without an article, it's often not clear to English speakers whether *die Sprache* (lit. "the language") refers to a specific language or to language in general. The same is true of *die Ideen*/"(the) ideas." Thus when Marx writes in (a) "Die Ideen existieren nicht getrennt von der Sprache," Nicolaus has to decide whether "*The* ideas [that we're talking about] do not exist separately from *the* language [that we're talking about]" or "*Ideas* do not exist separately from *language*." Obviously he opted for the latter, and I agree with that choice.

But then when Marx writes in (b>c) "die Analogie liegt dann aber nicht in der Sprache, sondern in ihrer Fremdheit," Nicolaus starts losing track. I think in opting for (b) "the language" he is guessing in the right direction—it is a specific language this time—but I would say that in English "the" is too vague. It leaves the English target reader wondering *which* language? In fact Marx is referring back to *eine fremde Sprache* "a foreign language": we need the specification of "*that* language," or even "that *foreign* language."

But the real problem arises in (c) *sondern in ihrer Fremdheit*, which is literally "but in her foreignness," again referring to that same foreign language—and yet for some reason Nicolaus changes course mid-stream, and renders that "but in the foreign quality *of language*."

Throughout that (b>c) second sentence Marx is referring to a single language, any specific target language into which ideas are translated, and arguing that the analogy he wants to construct between the circulation of ideas from one language to another and the circulation of commodities from one market or economy to another is *in the foreignness of the target language/economy*. It's not the foreignness of language in general.

So when Lydia Liu (1999: 22), who has no German, finds herself having to trust Nicolaus's translation, as a poststructuralist theorist she also finds herself powerfully attracted to the idea that *language itself*, all language, is "foreign":

> The foreign quality (*Fremdheit*) of language describes a shared process of circulation in translation and in economic transaction, which produces meaning as it produces value when a verbal sign of a commodity is exchanged with something foreign to itself.

> Marx's insistence on the foreignness (*Fremdheit*) of language is central to his working out of a meaningful connection between linguistic estrangement (*Entfremdung*) and monetary alienation (*Entäußerung*) in *Capital.*

I'm not sure what "the foreignness of language" would entail. Perhaps Sakai Naoki's (1997) "attitude of the heterolingual address," in which we are all foreigners to each other and to ourselves, so that we are always translating?

Maybe—though Sakai's model posits the foreignness not of "language" but of address, specifically as a situated rhetorical relationality between addressers and addressees.

And in any case that's not what Marx wrote.

2r

In my summary of this translation history and its impact on translational economic theory, therefore, I worked to narrow the interpretive scope available to us—to *exclude* misleading translations and translational misreadings.

But now let us throw open the interpretive gates to that "unruly hold-all of the manifold" by djreamifying the passage with Joycean portmanteaux, thereby perhaps tossing a wrench into the works. We start with a literal translation:

> (The) ideas exist not separated from (the) language. Ideas, that out of their mother tongue first into a foreign language translated must be, in order to circulate, in order exchangeable to become, offer already more analogy; the analogy however then lies not in (the) language, but in her foreignness.

The parenthetical "(the)" in its triple appearance obviously marks the target text for target-readerly choice: the specific ideas/language we're talking about, or ideas/language in general? The third "(the)" is obviously the interesting one, because it could really go either way: the obvious syntactic logic of target-language>analogy>target-language would seem to favor (b) "the language," and Nicolaus agreed; but a quantum leap from a specific target language to language in general is also possible, and Nicolaus apparently thought that was the most pressing corrective for (c) *in ihrer Fremdheit* "in her foreignness" ("her" literally because *die Sprache* "(the) language" is grammatically feminine).

But of course (c) the possessive pronoun *ihrer*/her is not the place to make that decision. (b) *Die Sprache*/(the) language is.

2s

In any case, then we start djreamifying it, using superscripts alongside portmanteaux for "unruly hold-all" inclusivity:

> (Dee)ideer (hex)ist not (in)separate from (dee)tunge. Ideer that out of (their)monthertunge fyrsty into (a)furrintunge transl(ou)ted muste bee, in larder to circumlout, in(law)order (hex)changehubble to becomb, offer (al)reedy (ever)more analyogie; (die)analyog(ie) however then lyes not in (die)(furrin)tunge, but in her (tungsten)furrinhite.

Let translation scholars with no German read *that* "wrong"!

2t

Some notes:

(dee) and (die) obviously blur the boundary between German and English, as Joyce too so often does in the *Wake*: "die" would normally be [di:] in German and [daɪ] in English, and the English pronunciation would signal not the definite article but an extraneous dying; but the double appearance of "(dee)" preceding "(die)" could possibly prime the target reader to read "die" as [di:], which is obviously also a recognized dialect pronunciation of "the" ("defeat of deduct went over defense before detail").

"not (in)separate" doubles the negation, or half-doubles it (and half-negates the doublin[6]), and so confuses the issue. Should the superscript "(in)" be ignored? Like "(dee)" and "(die)," it's obviously marked for choice, so the target reader can go either way (or both, or neither).

"(their)monthertunge" and "(a)furrintunge" implicitly (djreamily) expand the "unruly hold-all" of "language" from the traditional

6 A callback to Joyce's portmanteauing of Jonathan Sawyer's Dublin (section 2j above).

mother/foreign-tongue binary to time (“month”) and black hairy tongue syndrome (“furrin”).

As we’ve seen Fritz Senn noting wryly (section 2a), “Such stray semantemes, tangential possibilities, are an intrinsic hazard of the lexical wide sweep” (2013: 132). Experimental translation sweeps caustic lexical “lyes” into the taste buds of the mo(n)ther tongue and builds up dead skin cells that make that tongue blackly “furrin.” The furrin quality of literal/metaphorical tongues describes a shared process of circulation in experimental translation and mouth hygiene.

The insertion of “(tungsten)” as an expansion of *in ihrer Fremdheit* “in her foreignness” jostles Marx’s possessive-pronoun formulation to make room for Nicolaus’s “corrective”—“in the *foreign quality* of language”—and thus for Liu’s poststructuralist reading, with her dutiful acknowledgment of Shell’s German insertion “[*Fremdheit*],” as “the foreign quality (*Fremdheit*) of language” and “the foreignness (*Fremdheit*) of language” on which *Marx* supposedly insists. “Tungsten” unpacks as “tongue’s ten,” the first part of which might be read as “of language.” *Might*: the Joycean djreamlike distortion of idiomaticity makes that term not nearly as vulnerable to “misreading” as “of language.”

“fyrsty” is Joyce (*FW* 328.20).

“hubble” in “(hex)changehubble” is an allusion to the Hubble Space Telescope, which serves as a kind of astronomical knowledge exchange in earth orbit. “(hex)” of course, here and in “(hex)ist,” suggests witchcraft and thus a (hex)tension with scientific knowledge exchanges.

2u

But now what is the “djream” of “djreamish”? To what extent is the supposed djreaminess of the *Wake* just an oneiric metaphor signaling some kind of distortion of conventional (“waking”) language-logic?

In “*Finnegans Wake*: A Dream of Joyce—and its Real” Howard Rouse (2020) tracks Jacques Lacan’s engagement with the *Wake* from the “Joyce the Symptom” lecture at the fifth international Joyce Symposium in 1975 to the third section of the 1976 lecture that Jacques-Alain Miller titled “The Invention of the Real” and collected along with the earlier Joyce talk in *Seminar XXIII: Le/The Sinthome* (2005; Price 2016 in English).

Lacan was underwhelmed by Joyce’s djream-narrative. In fact he called Joyce’s conception of the djream “feeble-minded” (Price 148). For him the pluralization and blurring together of characters, especially of course HCE, was too reminiscent of the Jungian collective unconscious. Back in "Joyce the Symptom" Lacan had pointed out that Joyce plays on Jung as "Yung Pigeschoolies" (*FW* 100.6) and, a few pages later, refers to " 'alices, when they were yung and easily freudened" (115.24-25), which Lacan rejoyces as "s'il a 'freudened', s'il a freudenedé ce fredonnement" (in A.R. Price's English translation, "while he freudened this *fredonnement*, it was with repugnance," 2016: 143).

"Freudened," of course, sounds like "frightened" in English and like "fredonnement" (humming) in French.

In Chapter 4 of this book we find Walter Benjamin's frequent references to *die Freiheit* "(the) freedom" portmanteaued as "friedem" (German *Fried* "peace"/English "fried" + " 'em"), "friedum" ("fried" + "dumb"), "freodomity" ("freon" + Russian дом/*dom* "house"/ English "dom[inate etc.]"), "friodom" (Romance languages' *frio* "cold" + "dom"), "fleadom" (fleabag, fleahouse, etc.)—but also as "freedonement," alluding to this passage in Lacan.

So what exactly from Lacan's point of view was wrong with the Jungian conception?

2v

As is typical of Lacanian theory, it's complicated.[7]

It has to do with what Lacan theorized as the Borromean knot of the imaginary, the symbolic, and the real—a Borromean knot being a chaining of three rings so that severing one of them separates all three.

Three rings as three Viconian cycles—but Joyce severs them, cuts them up, repeats them piecemeal, without symmetry, without circular closure, without stable links. Given Lacan's insistence in *The Sinthome* that psychosis is the unraveling of the Borromean knot, for him in *Finnegans Wake* Joyce is courting psychosis.

And as Rouse (2020: n.p.) points out, there are indeed moments in the novel that seem to teeter on the verge of psychosis:

> In the last chapter of Book III, for example, Shem and Shaun, the twin sons of Earwicker and his wife Anna Livia Plurabelle,

7 For fuller discussions of the complications, see Schlossmann (2017) and Rouse (2020).

disintegrate into their own genesis in the parental coitus. Even more strikingly, in the book's final chapter, the sons are reabsorbed into the mother's (both *mère* and *mer* here) bodily fluid and the mother/wife into the ocean-like semen of her father.

Lacan adds that the psychotic unraveling of the Borromean knot can be prevented by the adding of the sinthome as a fourth ring; and according to Lacan Joyce's sinthome in the *Wake* is the Jungian collective unconscious. Lacan defined the sinthome as the subject's creative identification with the symptom; for both Jung and Joyce, according to Lacan, the rich but chaotic notion of the collective unconscious was that creative identification with the symptomatology of psychosis.[8] That enabled a potential cure for psychosis, but, tellingly, without an analytic to protect the subject (especially outside of analysis) from the plunge ever deeper into the psychotic break.

2w

Strikingly, this sinthomatic moment informs the deep mystical core of Walter Benjamin's "Aufgabe" as well, and figures in the pop quiz of this book's fourth chapter (p. 102):

> Eben darum wohnt in ihnen vor andern die ungeheure und ursprüngliche Gefahr aller Übersetzung: daß die Tore einer so erweiterten und durchwalteten Sprache zufallen und den Übersetzer ins Schweigen schließen. Die Sophokles-Übersetzungen waren Hölderlins letztes Werk. In ihnen stürzt der Sinn von Abgrund zu Abgrund, bis er droht in bodenlosen Sprachtiefen sich zu verlieren.
>
> Benjamin 1923/1972: 21

In Hölderlin's translouterments of Pindar and Sophocles lurches the most appaultorrific primoridipairil of all translouterdom: that when the sprogtorgates have been so silvatically sprong they may slamp shunt and enfowl the translouter in satournity. The metapozi of *Antigone* and *Oedipus Rex* were Hölderlin's last work. In

8 Jung (1952/1975: 116–17) too famously compared the language of Joyce's late work to schizophasic discourse.

> them manoing plonges from abbozzom to abbozzom until it risks pershwing in the bozzomless sprogpit.

Steering sinthomatically close to the psychotic edge allows Hölderlin to achieve transhuman perfection in translation—and teetering on that edge causes his "sense" to fall, topple, "plunge from abyss to abyss," silencing his poetic voice. The supreme creative engagement with psychosis supremely psychotizes creativity. As Jacques Derrida (1985: 234 in French, 203-4 in English) theorizes that moment:

> Depuis cette limite, à la fois intérieure et extérieure, le traducteur en vient à recevoir tous les signes de l'éloignement (Entfernung) qui le guide en sa démarche infinie, au bord de l'abîme, de la folie et du silence : les dernières œuvres de Hölderlin comme traductions de Sophocle, l'effondrement du sens "d'abîme en abîme", et ce danger n'est pas celui de l'accident, c'est la traductibilité, c'est la loi de la traduction, l'àtraduire comme loi, l'ordre donné, l'ordre reçu – et la folie attend des deux côtés. Et comme la tâche est impossible aux abords du texte sacré qui vous l'assigne, la culpabilité infinie vous absout aussitôt.

> From this limit, at once interior and exterior, the translator comes to receive all the signs of remoteness (Entfernung) which guide him on his infinite course, at the edge of the abyss, of madness and of silence: the last works of Hölderlin as translations of Sophocles, the collapse of meaning "from abyss to abyss," and this danger is not that of accident, it is transferability, it is the law of translation, the to-be-translated as law, the order given, the order received—and madness waits on both sides. And as the task is impossible at the approaches to the sacred text which assigns it to you, the infinite guilt absolves you immediately.

2x

Of course James Joyce did not suffer that fate—though some psychiatrists of his day claimed he did, and according to Robert Kaplan (2002: 172) he sailed closer to it than he might have liked.

One psychiatrist, Kaplan reports, "referred to him as the schizoid origin of his daughter's insanity" (172)—hebephrenic schizophrenia—and he was in a sense surrounded by mental illness all his adult life: his mother died in delirium, and his daughter-in-law suffered from bipolar disorder.

2y

Friedrich Hölderlin didn't suffer that fate either, in fact. He was diagnosed with a psychotic disorder in 1797, three years before he translated Pindar and seven years before he translated Sophocles, and he lived and wrote poetry for another four decades after his *Antigone* and *Oedipus Rex* were published. But it's a powerful image nonetheless—a Dark Romanticism of the imagination.

And of course the difference is that Walter Benjamin and Jacques Derrida were not in the business of curing psychosis. For them this all remained a literary *mythos*, an evocative story.

As a psychoanalyst, though, Jacques Lacan was in that business, and for him Jung's inability to use the collective unconscious analytically to cure psychosis was a major strike against his mystical alternative to Freudian psychoanalysis.

And so ultimately Lacan had the same beef with Joyce. Because Joyce's sinthome "doesn't tie on to anything," he says, *Finnegans Wake* "doesn't stir any sympathy in us" (2016: 131).

"In following Joyce," he writes in "Joyce as Symptom," "we are in the end exhausted," and that is "only the proof of the fact that our own symptoms are the only thing that hold any interest for each of us. The symptom in Joyce is a symptom that doesn't concern you at all. It's the symptom insofar as there is no chance that it hooks you up to something of your unconscious" (145).

"In the end exhausted": a dire prognosis for the experimental translator as well.

"Benjamins Totin' Vodka" is nowhere near as long as *Finnegans Wake*; but it doesn't take 600 pages to exhaust a reader.

2z

So what *are* the implications of Lacan's reservations for our project here, translouting that gaswind into djreamish? Is experimental translation psychotic? Is it pointless because it has no curative effect on psychosis?

Well, obviously not. Like Walter Benjamin and Jacques Derrida, and unlike Jacques Lacan, the experimental translator has no professional mandate to cure psychosis.

The tenuous links among dream, literature, and psychosis do, however, nudge the ethos of experimental translations a few notches upwards from cute but gratuitous verbal weirdness into a risky engagement with the embodied pushes and pulls of rationalist discipline and avant-garde disruptions.

In previous work on experimental translation I have tended to stress the light it can cast on the traditional equivalence-based norms of translation—(loutishly) aggravating the target reader into reluctant reflection on the repressed idealizations of translation, and the paradoxes and impossibilities that they safeguard. This engagement with Lacan on Joyce suggests that the target reader's reluctant reflections may more broadly engage the repressed idealizations not just of translation but of sanity as a social norm and construct.

3 Heteronymous Translouters

As far as I can tell, the first (and perhaps only?) critic to apply the term "heteronym" to Joyce's work was Max Saunders in Chapters 7–8 of *Self Impression: Life-Writing, Autobiografiction, and the Forms of Modern Literature* (2010).

As we'll see, however, all that was really new in Saunders' take on Joyce was the term.

The idea that *Ulysses* and *A Portrait of the Artist as a Young Man* and even three stories in *Dubliners* were "actually" (fictitiously, heteronymously) written by Stephen Dedalus has been around for a long time; and according to Saunders it is hinted in *Finnegans Wake* (125.23) that Shem the Penman is the whole novel's heteronymous author.

But let's step back.

3a

"Heteronym" (*heteronímia*) is a concept named and defined and extensively used by the great Portuguese modernist poet Fernando Pessoa (1888–1935), a slightly younger contemporary of James Joyce (1882–1941), to mean a characterized stand-in for the author—a "pseudonym" or othered voice with a detailed backstory, a distinct style and technique, a history of literary influence, and a complexly layered relationship with other heteronyms.

It has been variously estimated that Pessoa created and used over a hundred such heteronyms—not only poets and prose writers but journalists, editors, philosophers, and translators.

DOI: 10.4324/9781003470427-3

One of his heteronyms in fact was named Fernando Pessoa: a self-fictionalization, which of course is quite common in literature—and, as Max Saunders points out, in life—but in this as in most other areas Pessoa takes imposture to a greater extreme than anyone else, "disintegrating both principles invoked in that expression: possession, and kind" (304).

Pessoa, in other words, disavowed both that his heteronyms were *like* him and that they *were* him. The rest of us tend to stuff all our various personalities (roama)loosely into the portmanteau that we call "me."

3b

In a Romantic "expressive theory of art," Saunders notes, "art that tries to express another personality than the author's is a kind of fake. But if a dramatist or a novelist can fake a convincing unconscious life as well as a convincing 'inner life' for a character, why could he or she not also fake a character producing a creative work?" (304).

One counterargument to the Romantic view, in other words, is that there is a "creative mystery" to all artistic impostures, including the Romantic expressivist kind. Saunders himself leans in the opposite direction:

> The other counter-argument agrees that there is no essential difference [between Romantic and heteronymous impostures], but pursues it to the opposite conclusion. Rather than seeing heteronymic speech as being as much a creative mystery as heteronymic writing, it sees both as comparable forgeries. This is the post-structuralist view, according to which all discourse is essentially heteronymic, in that it doesn't express us, but itself. According to this view, heteronymity is just deconstruction by other means.
>
> Saunders 2010: 305

3c

Saunders devotes the better part of two chapters, 7 and 8, to a careful analysis of heteronymity in Joyce. For some reason, however, his discussion of *Ulysses* and *Finnegans Wake* is limited to a handful of passing references; only *A Portrait of the Artist as a Young Man* receives a close analysis aimed at identifying (potential or notional) heteronymity.

Saunders argues that reading *A Portrait* as written by Stephen, and therefore as a heteronymous novel, solves the problem around which a good deal of the critical literature on the novel resolves, namely whether the older Joyce's portrait of Stephen as the younger Joyce is sincere or ironic, and, if the latter, whether it is ironic enough:

> This distinction misses what might be Joyce's most ingenious strategy, which is to construct a text that can be read as if it were the novel written by its protagonist, thus encapsulating the autobiographical reading (though in a fictionalized mode) within the ironic. It could thus be another example of the games we know Joyce enjoyed playing with his interpreters.
>
> Saunders 2010: 300

"Might be," "can be," "could be": the rather extreme conditionality of this reading makes Joyce's first novel an odd choice for extended analysis.

And it is through his notional reading of *A Portrait* that Saunders introduces the concept of the heteronym: "To read Stephen Dedalus as the book's fictional author is to read him as an example of what the great Portuguese modernist Fernando Pessoa called a 'heteronym'" (303).

One is tempted to say *no, not exactly*, because Stephen is not explicitly identified as the novel's author, or even as its narrator.

Indeed Saunders himself seems to lean this way as well, as a few lines later he asks whether the difference between a pseudonym and a heteronym is that "a heteronym in Pessoa's sense needs to be known to be a fictional performance" (303–4).

He doesn't attempt to answer his own question.

3d

Saunders cheerfully admits that his reading of *A Portrait* is both farfetched when narrowed to a fine point (Stephen Dedalus wrote the book) and patently obvious when sufficiently generalized (Stephen Dedalus can usefully be imagined as the narrator and perhaps even fictional author of the book).

He argues, however, that a heteronymizing reading of *A Portrait* helps us frame Joyce's whole career in new ways: "If it seems far-fetched, it seems less so if we approach Joyce's career backwards. We know the idea attracted him later. *Finnegans Wake* is presented as written by one of its fictional characters, 'Shem the Penman'" (314).

And he backtracks the emergence in Joyce of a heteronymizing approach to fiction-writing, from his experience of reading *La coscienza di Zeno* by his English student Italo Svevo in early 1924 (possibly an influence on the *Wake*), back to arguments that Stephen wrote *Ulysses* and *A Portrait*, and then all the way back to the fact that three of the stories in *Dubliners* were originally published under the pseudonym of Stephen Dedalus.

Arguably Stephen begins as a pseudonym and is gradually, through the writing of *Stephen Hero, A Portrait of the Artist as a Young Man*, and *Ulysses*, rendered heteronymous.

3e

But now, the *Wake*. Does the text really "present" Shem as the novel's heteronymous author? The passage Saunders cites is at the end of Chapter I-5:

> Not Hans the Curier though had he had have only had some little laughings and some less of cheeks and were he not so warried by his bulb of persecussion he could have, ay, and would have, as true as Essex bridge. And not Gopheph go gossip, I declare to man! Noe! To all's much relief one's half hypothesis of that jabberjaw ape amok the showering jestnuts of Bruisanose was hotly dropped and his room taken up by that odious and still today insufficiently malestimated notesnatcher (kak, pfooi, bosh and fiety, much earny, Gus, poteen? Sez you!) Shem the Penman.
>
> *FW* 125.14–23

For what deed is the narrator trying to identify the doer there? Writing the novel?

No: writing a letter.

3f

It is, of course, a pretty momentous letter.

In a footnote (314n52) Saunders cites Tindall (1959: 274) on that letter, saying that Joyce "demonstrates a comparable use of *mise en abyme*, involving a framed letter written down by Shem (in *Finnegans Wake*, pp. 104–25): 'Dictated by A.L.P. and addressed to H.C.E., the letter was written by Shem the Penman and carried by Shaun the Post. The letter, we gather, is an epitome of *Finnegans Wake* and, like it, is at once simple and baffling.'"

But is the fictional author of a letter that "we gather" is an "epitome" or *mise en abîme* of *Finnegans Wake* automatically on that basis to be regarded as the fictional author of *Finnegans Wake*?

No. "*Finnegans Wake* is [NOT] presented as written by" Shem.[1]

So what is the relevance of heteronyms here?

Well, Shem is arguably (but abyssally) the heteronymous author of that letter. He may not be presented as having written the entire novel, but he is absented as a heteronymous writer—one notionally characterized in a way that makes him seem like Joyce's alter ego ("other(ed)-I," in the sense of *not-Joyce*).

3g

So do we have a narratorial presence that we might plausibly/deniably identify as a heteronymous author of the whole novel?

In a way, yes. Joyce scholars have come to call that figure "the dreamer"—the dream-narrator (or djream-narrator), at the very least, and according to many the fictional author as well.

Joyce, in other words, was not *imitating* or *pretending to write* a dream-narrative. He was letting the djreamer narrate the djream through him.

Accordingly, some scholars have argued that the djreamer was Joyce himself, or Joyce's unconscious mind. Joyce himself famously

1 To the extent that the letter is a *mise en abîme*, of course, or calquingly a *putting in abyss/chasm/hell*, an insertion into an infinit(esimalit)y of thought, an abyssal wager, its epitomizing force is negative, kenotic, an emptying or occultation or absenting of narrative coherence. The letter sucks reassuring premodernity/discipline/order out of the novel. It's not *written* by Shem; it's *not-written* by an absent not-Shem. It's not-carried by an absent not-Shaun. It's not-dictated by an absent not-ALP. It's not-about an absent not-HCE. It's not-heard by an absent nonjudge and nonjury (adding nonsult to nonjury). And so on.

In all those negative senses, it is a useful epitome of the novel. But its abyssality would seem to empty out all such confident positive claims as "*Finnegans Wake* is presented as written by one of its fictional characters, 'Shem the Penman'" (Saunders 2010: 314). If anything it's absented as not-written by none of its fictional characters.

denied it: “Really it is not I who am writing this crazy book. It is you, and you, and you, and that man over there, and that girl at the next table” (quoted by Kenner 1987: 327, who is quoted by Chrisp 2016: n.p.).

Peter Chrisp adds that the *Wake* makes this “distributed” or pluralized authorship clear throughout: “brings *us* by a commodius vicus of recirculation back to Howth Castle and Environs” (3.2), “*we* are back” (30.3), “*we* all know Anna Livia” (196.3), and so on. “In fact,” Chrisp adds, “all the first five chapters use ‘us’ or ‘we’ by the ninth line at the latest—and the sixth chapter ends ‘Semus sumus.’ We are Shem. All of us.”

We are all Joyce’s heteronyms?

3h

Some scholars argue that the *Wake* is a dream without a dreamer. But there is a voice narrating the djream, and that voice has certain obsessive concerns—not the detailed backstory, distinct style and technique, history of literary influence, and so on that I said Pessoa’s heteronyms have, but enough repetitive intensity of focus that it is reasonable to call it/him/her/them/us a characterized heteronym.

Philip Kitcher (2009), for example, goes on at considerable length to describe that character: he’s an aging man, someone who fears his best days are past; his focus is no longer what it used to be; his days of sexual pleasure are largely past, and so on. He’s a married man, and, like HCE, his marriage has seen better days as well.

Some scholars assume that HCE is the dreamer, and certainly HCE is “the dreamer’s central locus of identification” (Kitcher 2013: 52); “this, however,” Kitcher argues, “might blind us to the ways in which the dreamer’s response to the vignettes can depend on identification with figures distinct from, even opposed to, HCE” (51).

In Kitcher’s reading the dreamer conjures up HCE as a kind of characterized alter ego by way of exploring his existential concerns, especially by putting HCE in problematic situations, like being accused of doing something unsavory with two girls in the park, and being an outsider who doesn’t fit in, and so on.

And then he conjures up ALP as a wifely foil to HCE, a female understanding of HCE, with lingering love but also decades of disappointment. And then he imagines their children, the twins Shaun and Shem and their little sister Issy. And more and more characters keep getting added to the djream-narrative, townspeople, characters from myth and legend, literary figures like Tristan and Isolde, historical heroes, the four evangelists, a donkey, all not merely as foils but as upward and downward streamers of the lightning of story-telling creativity.

The djreamer as the novel's primary heteronymous author, characterized but unnamed; HCE as the next heteronymous emanation; then ALP; then the kids; then here comes everybody.

As Kitcher notes at one point, "There are many ways of questioning that vision, and it is important for anyone drawn to realizing it to confront those questions—if the prosecutor did not exist, Shem would have to invent him. The prosecutor lives within Shem—as Shem and ALP live within HCE—or, better, as all these voices live within the dreamer at the Wake" (40).

3i

So now how might heteronyms be mobilized by the experimental translator?

As it happens, this is a question to which I have explored answers as a translation scholar, in Chapter 4 of *The Experimental Translator* (2023c), Question 6 of *Questions for Translation Studies* (2023e), and *Translator, Touretter* (2024b: sections 3w-y, 4v-x); as an experimental translator, in my transcreation of Volter Kilpi's *Gulliver's Voyage to Phantomimia* (2020) and my earlier translations of Walter Benjamin's "Aufgabe" (2023a, 2024b); and as a novelist, both in my pseudotranslation of J.I. Vatanen's *The Last Days of Maiju Lassila* (2022b) and in *Insecticide: A Republican Romance* (2024a).[2]

Because I have tracked those experiments at some length before, and because I offer a longer and more explicitly Joycean/*Wake*an

2 In *Insecticide* "Douglas 'Dogfish' Robinson" the heteronymous author and "William 'Billfish' Kaul" his heteronymous researcher die just before the ending, of an apparent overdose of ivermectin; conspiracy theorists are inclined to blame a Bush family hit for their untimely deaths. By this point in the novel's plot, in late 1999, two and a half decades before its actual publication, the novel *Insecticide* is a runaway global bestseller that has sold more copies than the Bible; "Dogfish" and "Billfish" are given heteronymous personalities, professional backgrounds, and mutually hostile families who nevertheless join forces to sue McDonald's for breach of contract in the creation of *Insecticide*-themed Happy Meal toys. (Bill is an old friend of mine who did in fact work on the creation of the novel.)

experiment in Chapter 4, I'll sketch the heteronymity of my Kilpi and Vatanen books quickly and superficially here.

3j

The Kilpi transcreation was inspired by my realization that Kilpi himself had written it through two heteronyms: Lemuel Gulliver as the author and Volter Kilpi as the translator.

Kilpi had followed Jonathan Swift in setting Gulliver up as the fictional author, but was forced to add a step by the fact that while Swift wrote his novel in the same language as the fictional author's native tongue, English, he (Kilpi) wrote his in Finnish, a language alien to the eighteenth-century English-speaking author-heteronym. He solved that problem by heteronymizing himself as the translator.

And my initial idea was that I could follow Kilpi in heteronymizing Gulliver as the author and then, since I have the same first language as Gulliver, heteronymizing myself as the book's *editor*. I would actually translate it, but pretend to have found the same manuscript in English and edited it.

But then it occurred to me that as editor "I" (my editorial heteronym) would have found either a partial manuscript, corresponding to just the twenty-four and a half chapters that Kilpi wrote before his death, or the whole manuscript, which would require that I write the ending of the novel that Kilpi had told his son he was planning.

There was really no contest, though: the latter option sounded like a lot more fun.

3k

What I found in writing the ending, however, was that I couldn't match the style and tone of my translation of Kilpi's unfinished text. My ending was much more Swiftian-satirical than anything Kilpi wrote; his was much more philosophical than mine. What to do?

I decided that for the part that I was translating from Kilpi my editor-heteronym would take Jonathan Swift as its second-tier author-heteronym (behind the Gulliver author-heteronym) and for my continuation would speculate variously about the "actual" author (a second second-tier author-heteronym): Captain Samuel Brunt, the pseudonymous author of *A Voyage to Cacklogallinia* (1727)? Edmund Halley (1656-1741)?

Or, perhaps, since my continuation is manifestly more Swiftian than what Kilpi wrote—not just more satirical but more humorously sacrilegious (Kilpi was a devout Christian, Swift a notoriously freethinking cleric)—perhaps "Swift" wrote my continuation and someone else wrote the first twenty-four and a half chapters?

31

But then, as I translated and wrote along, a slew of paratextual pranks began to occur to me. (I later realized that they were unconsciously inspired by memories of my favorite novel, Vladimir Nabokov's *Pale Fire*. I'm not sure why I didn't recognize that source immediately.)

What if my editor-heteronym were to footnote the "original English manuscript" copiously, supposedly in an effort to explain it *as* an original eighteenth-century script but actually, by pointing out egregious anachronisms and self-contradictions, undermining that impression?

What if I were to write an editor's preface in which the "Douglas Robinson" editor-heteronym was confused and disturbingly paranoid, convinced that shadowy forces were stalking him, attempting to steal the precious manuscript?

What if I were to invent a bellicose Finnish critic-heteronym who angrily accused me of "stealing" Kilpi's posthumous novel by adding all this heteronymous material?

Since the novel revolves around a time-traveling polar vortex, what if I were to have Ezra Pound or Wyndham Lewis (poet-heteronyms) discover the same English manuscript in 1914 and be inspired by it to launch Vorticism?

What if I were to transform Ethel Cartwright, in the novel the 15-year-old son of the skipper—the ingenious one who comes up with and successfully implements the plan to steal an airplane and fly it back around the polar vortex to take them home to England in 1738—into a thirty-something time-traveler who has engineered this entire multigenerational endeavor, secreting the Gulliver manuscript first to Pound or Wyndham Lewis, then to Kilpi, then to Deleuze and Guattari, then to me? The paratextual Ethel is a publisher-heteronym; at the end of his Publisher's Postscript he admits that he too, like the vituperous Finnish critic-heteronym, was invented by Douglas Robinson (the "real" one? who knows!?).

3m

"So you didn't actually translate the novel," friends say when I tell this story.

"Of course I translated the novel," I reply. "I just situated that translation in a larger creative context that made it a 'transcreation.'" And the multiple mutually undermining heteronyms largely power that larger creative context.

And in fact the bellicose Finnish critic-heteronym "himself" admits grudgingly that I did it pretty accurately, though with the "superfluous" "embellishments" of eighteenth-century Swiftian lexicon, punctuations, and capitalizations.

3n

In a way my experimental play with heteronyms is simpler in my pseudotranslation of J.I. Vatanen's *The Last Days of Maiju Lassila*, in that I did in it what Kilpi did in his *Gulliver*: I wrote a novel and pretended to have translated it. That simple premise is complicated, however, by several twists.

One is that I launch the same play with footnotes in the novel as I'd done in the Kilpi transcreation: as the translator-heteronym I try repeatedly, in footnote after footnote, to verify and establish the 1922 writing date supposedly scribbled in pencil on the title page of the (imaginary) manuscript supposedly stored in the Finnish National Library—and, as in *Gulliver*, end up "discovering" (actually, inventing and strategically planting) all manner of anachronisms that undermine the illusion.

The footnotes, in other words, are stretched across the skin between "translation" and "pseudotranslation"—between "written by J.I. Vatanen and translated by Douglas Robinson" and "written and only pseudotranslated by Douglas Robinson."

3o

That stretchiness drove the book's *Kirkus* reviewer out of his tiny mind with frustrated rage (kirkusreviews.com/book-reviews/ji-vatanen/the-last-days-of-maiju-lassila/): "In short, Robinson ensures the reader is always lost and makes it clear this is his intention in the preface to the book, a literary approach with a long pedigree the author dutifully acknowledges. So what precisely is the point of deploying a derivative literary technique to tell an unintelligible story that lacks dramatic power?"[3]

3p

Another twist is that *as characters* J.I. Vatanen and Maiju Lassila are themselves heteronyms—heteronyms created by the Finnish novelist Algot Untola (1878–1918).

Untola published one novel under the J.I. Vatanen heteronym and 15 novels and five plays under the Maiju Lassila heteronym; so popular was the Maiju Lassila heteronym that to this day Untola is still often referred to as Maiju Lassila.

What I did was to make four of Untola's heteronyms and Untola himself (mainly in fact his revenant) characters in the novel and use the narrative to explore author-heteronym relations.

Untola died in the water off Helsinki, shot after being pushed off the transport ship in which he was being ferried to his execution as a Red agitator after the conclusion of the Finnish Civil War in May 1918.

In my novel, in the aftermath of that shooting he is given another nine months to roam the earth, and during that time Maiju and the other heteronym under whose name he published extensively, Irmari Rantamala, develop excruciating pain in the exact places of his bullet holes: intergenerational trauma, rethought through heteronymity.

3q

It is a truism among translation scholars that the translator has no access to the "I" and so cannot perform speech acts (Malmkjær 1988: 35–36; Pym 1993; see Robinson 2003: 137–38 for discussion).

My counterargument[4] has long been that while traditional translators are technically incapable of performing *direct* speech acts—"I warn you," "I baptize you," "I declare the conference open," etc.—they can nevertheless perform indirect speech acts, and especially are

3 For a rejoinder to this *Kirkus* numbskullery that eloquently lays out more or less the exact opposite reading, and in fact is strongly aligned with the counterpositions I explore in this book, see Riley (2023).

4 See e.g. Robinson (2016: 76–77; 2017a: 37–39; 2017c: 116–26; 2017d: 85–115; 2019: 189–98; 2022c: 102–119).

entirely available to participate in what Eve Sedgwick (2003: 67–91) calls periperformativity, the swarm of audience indirect speech acts that ratify or refuse to ratify (or more often complexly semiratify) performatives.

But it is a whole new ballgame for experimental translators, who do not have to hide behind invisibility norms; they can play with what Boris Groys (2016) calls "their nominal identities as ready-mades":

> Here the question is not whether the true self is real or merely a metaphysical fiction. The question of identity is not a question of truth but a question of power: Who has the power over my own identity—I myself or society? And, more generally: Who exercises control and sovereignty over the social taxonomy, the social mechanisms of identification—state institutions or I myself? The struggle against my own public persona and nominal identity in the name of my sovereign persona or sovereign identity also has a public, political dimension because it is directed against the dominating mechanisms of identification—the dominating social taxonomy, with all its divisions and hierarchies. Later, these artists mostly gave up the search for the hidden, true self. Rather, they began to use their nominal identities as ready-mades—and to organize a complicated play with them. But this strategy still presupposes a disidentification from nominal, socially codified identities—with the goal of artistically reappropriating, transforming, and manipulating them. The politics of modern and contemporary art is the politics of nonidentity. Art says to its spectator: I am not what you think I am (in stark contrast to: I am what I am). The desire for nonidentity is, actually, a genuinely human desire—animals accept their identity but human animals do not.

Groys is writing about the artistic avant-garde. I am suggesting that translators too can join that advance guard, and have literary fun with nominal identities.

3r

First step: the translator is invisible and inaudible. The translator has no voice and no body. The translator is a nonhuman conduit of someone else's words and style: a window through which the target reader can see the source text clearly; a recording device with the help of which the target reader can hear the source author's voice clearly.

Second step: the translator has precisely as much voice as the source author does, and airs it in much the same way, indirectly, periperformatively. Literary scholars know that the authors of novels do not speak in their novels: narrators do. Narrators serve as authors' heteronymous stand-ins—though the so-called unreliable narrator is specifically created as a *foil* to the author's views.

It is possible for source authors to create a character called "the Author," or who carries the author's name, as I do in *Insecticide*; but when that character speaks, it's not the author speaking. It's the heteronym speaking "as" or "for" the author (often unreliably). In *Insecticide* "the Author" dies before the end of the novel, which is already a runaway bestseller a quarter century before its actual publication.

Traditional translators do the same, and that fact has been recognized by a substratum of Descriptive Translation Studies (beginning with Giuliana Schiavi 1996 and Theo Hermans 1996) that has come to be called the study of the translator as narrator (see Robinson 2022a for discussion).

Third step: experimental translators create heteronyms specifically in order to be able to play with nominal identities, to the end of stretching and twisting normative binaries like visible and invisible, audible and inaudible, reproductive and transformative, slavish and free, humble and brazen.

Their goal is not (necessarily) to flip those binaries—to make the invisible visible, the slavish free, the humble brazen, etc.—but to study them by putting them into productive tension with each other, and to parade their findings before target readers, to rub those readers' noses in the normally repressed awkwardnesses and discomfitures that the binaries have always produced.

And, of course, as we saw at the end of Chapter 2, to make target readers engage the shifting boundaries between sanity and psychosis.

3s

Finally a few words about Chapter 4, this book's showcase translation of Walter Benjamin's "Die Aufgabe des Übersetzers" as "Benjamins Totin' Vodka."

That title is a homophonic translauting of an imagined Benjaminesque adaptation of an imagined literal translation of Joyce's title into German as *Finnegans Totenwache.*

Dieter H. Stündel's 1993 full translation of the *Wake* into German did not translate "wake" as *Totenwache*, but *überlautete*/translauted Joyce's title as *Finnegans Wehg*—a portmanteau of German *Weh* "woe" and *weg* "(a)way," with the barest hint of "waking" in the implied homophone *weck*, the imperative of *wecken* "to wake someone up," as in *weck mich auf* "wake me up."

But if Stündel had translated "wake" into German as a noun, it would have been *Totenwache*.

Eine Totenwache in German is morphologically "a wake of the dead"; I playfully justify translauting that homophonically as "Totin' Vodka" in the piece by having the multiple authorial heteronyms tote some vodka.

3t

"Benjamins Totin' Vodka" is my fifth full (and by far the fullest, indeed overstuffed) translation of Benjamin's essay.

The first (2023a) was a paraphrase written for *Translation as a Form*; it was a little freer than a traditional sense-for-sense translation, on the grounds that Benjamin hated sense-for-sense translation, attacked it mercilessly in the "Aufgabe," and therefore that an explanatory translation aimed at conveying the ideas in the essay should not be conceived or presented as a quantitatively accurate transmission of the sense (sentential semantics) of the German source text.

Just above that paraphrase, therefore, at the head of each segment, I put an interlinear box, giving pride of place to the spatialized form that Benjamin himself called the prototype or ideal of all translation.

Those boxes originally contained Benjamin's German original and my second translation, a radical Hölderlinian etymological literal translation, based entirely on English cognates for Benjamin's German words. The reviewers for the press, though, called it self-indulgent nonsense (not entirely wrong), so I replaced those lines in the interlinear boxes with a third translation, a traditional literal one, such as is typically found in interlinears.

Once that book was accepted for publication, I began shopping the radical cognate translation around to journals, under a new cognate-based title: "Th' Upgiving o' th' O'ersetter." At first there were no takers; and then, when one journal agreed to build a forum around it, the editor kept it for a year and finally returned it, saying that he couldn't get anyone to respond to it.

3u

So I thought, you know, *sic semper*—until Alex Lukes emailed me, saying she was editing an essay collection titled *Avant-Garde Translation*, and could she possibly—?

She had read my *Asymptote* piece on avant-garde translation (Robinson 2021) and wanted to reprint it. I said yes, of course, but also sent her the Word preprint of what was then my forthcoming book *The Experimental Translator* (2023c) and "Th' Upgiving o' th' O'ersetter"—and things began to happen.

3v

Alex suggested that I incorporate the full Benjamin cognate translation into the article, and I was happy to do that.

She also passed word to Lily Robert-Foley about my forthcoming book, and a few days later Lily wrote to me asking if she could see the preprint; I sent it to her, and we struck up a lively email correspondence.

Then I was asked by Goldsmiths Press to review Lily's book *Experimental Translation* (2023) for publication, and it blew my mind even more than her 2020 article had done—and fed my imagination for the next stage of Benjamin (and other experimental) translation.

3w

The next step was that, based on *Translation as a Form,* Benjamin scholars in Europe asked me to coedit a centennial essay collection on Benjamin's "Aufgabe," and I agreed—and as I thought about possibly contributing to the volume, with Lily's book manuscript surging about in my head, what occurred to me was the fourth full translation, which I ended up giving the homophonic title "D'oof-gobble Dusk Over Seltzers" (2024b).

Maybe, I thought, this time I could venture a few steps *past* the Hölderlinian translation strategy that Benjamin lauds, and try something new? Maybe several new somethings?

I ended up trying out a different experimental translation strategy—paging through Lily's manuscript for inspiration—on each of Benjamin's eleven paragraphs, but two on his third paragraph, which begins with the fateful pronouncement "Die Übersetzung ist eine Form" (fateful not only in the sense that no one quite seems to know what it means, but because I adapted it for the title of my centennial commentary, *Translation as a Form*).

What to do with it? I offered it to my fellow coeditors, and they were not overly excited by the idea—and then Lily Robert-Foley wrote asking whether she could have it for the collection or compendium she and Delphine Grass were coediting titled *The Unending Lives of Translation: Creative-Critical Experiments in Translation and Life Writing* (Robinson 2025).

These weird textual experiments of mine that at first no one wanted were suddenly in demand!

3x

Why now a fifth? Is this now something I will do every year, turn out a new experimental translation of Benjamin's essay?[5]

I wouldn't rule that possibility out entirely; but for now this Joyce book got me thinking about the experimental possibilities for translation not only of homophonic translauting and the building of portmanteau words but of heteronyms, and I began to consider how to illustrate all three together.

It's one thing to have put authorial, translational, editorial, and otherial heteronyms to interesting use in my past work, as I've discussed in sections 3i-p; it's quite another to channel translautings, portmanteaux, and heteronyms into a whole new translouting.

5 I was asked recently why I have been so interested in Benjamin, writing a book-length commentary on and five full translations of his "Aufgabe," after initially hating it (Robinson 1996: 200-9). My answer was that studying the essay and its unstated backgrounds for *Translation as a Form* made me appreciate its radicalism more, and specifically its radical call for experimental translation (though Benjamin doesn't explicitly use that term). Something in the essay's mystical bombast began to have a weird attraction for me, and my imagination translated that appeal into translational experimentation.

3y

And so that is what I have done. As you'll see, I do the serial homophonic translautings in section 4a, from the first paragraph of Benjamin's German and then from a translation into a different language—French, Russian, Spanish, Chinese, and Finnish—of each of Benjamin's next five paragraphs.

I don't make my paragraph breaks align with Benjamin's; I have the Heedful Copy Editor (HCE) indicate the beginnings and ends of Benjamin's paragraphs (and the shifts to new intermediate languages) in footnotes.

And then, as HCE footnotes snarkily, I run out of languages that I am able to translaut from. That is the end of section 4a.

(HCE is one of the translation's heteronyms, named, obviously, though askew, after the main djream-character in *Finnegans Wake*.)

The six paragraphs of section 4a's homophonic translautings are also constantly being interrupted by the other heteronyms. Some of them are alter egos of Walter Bendix Schönflies Benjamin: Walt the Romantic, Bendix the Kneelplatoonist (Neoplatonist), Schönflies the Crabblist (Kabbalist), the Art Scholiast, and Benjy the Exhorticulturalist.

Benjamin's essay has been read as *fundamentally* Kabbalist, Neoplatonist, or Romantic, of course, and his exhortative reliance on horticultural metaphors for the messianic growth of languages toward the eschatology of pure language (the seed, the kernel, the stump and stalk, the fruit, the skin) has often been noted and discussed; what this proliferation of Benjaminian heteronyms achieves is not only a critical exploration of the intertwining of those perspectives but the actual interactive and interjective *voicing* of those perspectives.

Still other heteronyms are introduced as foils, based mostly on Benjamin's attacks on traditional thinking about translation: the Dead Theorist, the Superficial Thinker, the Elderly Translation Studies Scholar. Others are historical figures whom Benjamin cites, especially Duns Scotus, Wilhelm Dilthey, Rudolf Pannwitz, and Stéphane Mallarmé.

The Idiot Questioner, who asks the questions in section 4c's pop quiz, is of course another named heteronym, "characterized" not only through the attributive modifier "Idiot" and the initials IQ, but also through the disgruntled polemics in which they engage in the footnotes (invariably by asking idiot questions).

In the homophonic first section, whenever one of the heteronyms interjects and a conversation ensues, I drop out of translauting mode and slip into portmanteau words. Once I run out of foreign languages that I'm more or less (un)comfortable with, moving from the homophonic section 4a to sections 4b-c, I make the shift to translating entirely into portmanteau words.

In section 4b I use the page format of the kids studying upstairs in *FW* Chapter II.2 (pp. 260ff), ending with a "pome" (as poem and as apple), using the poem or song format of *FW* pp. 45–47.

Then in section 4c, as I began to suggest just above, I use the quiz format of *FW* pp. 126ff.

The study session in section 4b makes a fragmented kind of side dialogue possible, as the heteronyms annotate the translated text in three places, on the left and right hand and in the foot; and of course the copyeditor-heteronym HCE continues to comment as well, especially by glossing foreign words for "translation" and "language"; and sometimes the translauthor-heteronym DR too puts in their oar.

The left- and right-margin heteronym commentaries are phased out in section 4c's quiz, leaving only the footnotes for heteronymous dialogue; but as I say, IQ is especially pertinacious.

3z

Chapter 4 may be a showcase of Joyce-inspired experimental translation methods, and its playful mood is a lot closer to the *Wake* than to Benjamin's knit-browed "Aufgabe"; but it is not quite a pastiche of *Finnegans Wake*.

In fact it deviates from Joyce's novel in a number of significant ways, especially by building an explicit dialogue between the numerous named heteronyms and the variably translated text. (It channels something like the exchanges between heteronymous translator(s) and narrator(s) that Cervantes mustered in *Don Quixote*.)

While I argued in Chapter 2 that *Finnegans Wake* is everywhere a kind of displaced translational text, Joyce based it only very loosely and tangentially on a single source text, the street ballad "Finigan's Wake"; because "Benjamins Totin' Vodka" is not an experimental novel but an experimental translation, it moves djreamily but persistently through Benjamin's German "Aufgabe," beginning to end.

4 A Showcase of Joycean Experimental Translation

"Benjamins Totin' Vodka"[1]

4a

Serial Homophonic Translautings

— Let me chust shteit an oblovious und encontravourtible trouth, intound Waltder Romantiker: — that[2] near guns airviced sick eyenumb coonswork odor ionair coonsform gaygunuber d'rucksicked off deign oofneigh mendin' fir Derringer Kentness freakedbar.

— What!? yolped die Art Scholiar from acrost the odditorium, stuggering to his feat, eyen white.

1 "Totin' Vodka" seems to be a homophonic translauting of German *Totenwache*, or "wake" in the sense that Joyce's last novel is the "wake" of multiple Finnegans: the period between death and burial, usually accompanied by a party of some sort. The heteronymous partiers at "Benjamins Wake" are all dead but drinking vodka; but like Joyce's narrator and main characters—HCE, ALP, Shaun and Shem, Issy—they are also evidently djream figures who speak as or to or past the author himself, in various guises (in Benjamin the Romantic, the neo-Platonist, the Kabbalist, the Horticulturalist, etc.). The first page is mostly translauted homophonically from the first paragraph of Benjamin's German original, but speech attributions and interjected protests and arguments typically use Joyce's portmanteau style. I'll pop back in to indicate where that translauting-from-German shifts to translauting-from-French, and where each later shift occurs as well. [Heedful Copy Editor, aka HCE]
Note that the "HCE" who writes these notes is also a Joycean heteronym. [DR]
Note that the "DR" who added that last line is also a Joycean heteronym. [HCE]
There is no heteronym in Joyce with the initials DR. [DR]
There are no heteronyms in Joyce at all. They're *characters*. [HCE]

2 This is the beginning of the homophonic *Überlautung* (over allow tongue) from Benjamin's German, beginning with the first line of his essay. [HCE]
Your tongue's over its allowance. [DR]
Which is precisely the point. [HCE]

DOI: 10.4324/9781003470427-4

— It's nicked canoed, sagd Walt (dizzily), — doss yay-duh Betsy hung aw fine beigetimidness booblickem odor dressin' reppraisin' tauntin' foam vague upfirth; its cigar dare bagrift eyeness "e-day-all-in" offneighmendin' in Holland cooinstarearraytishin' aireartherrungin' foamable, vile diesel ladygleek gayhalten sinned, dawesine and vazin' dusk mention overhopped for owlzoosensin'.

— Well but come on, sagd die Art Scholiar, — Jeeze Louise, my groot man, I am Groot, so sets ouch dicundus cellbust dissin' loblickess und geisty guess vazin' for owls—zany owlsmixemkite auburn in kinda mere or fairkey.

— Okei, gut, sagd Waltder Romantiker, — but it doss knot rewire deir achtunghut! After oil, you vood agree, I archsume, that kine gaydicked guilt dame laser, kine build dame bayshower, gynesymphony dare whorrorshaft.[3] I mean, introduction votell poorly lectures key neo-con pregnant paw loreregional, am I right?

— I don't … begandy Art Scholiar.

— Sail a pure assembler suffearall hexplikay law differounced kneevoe enter lay dirt, dawnly domeman deliared? inqueeried the Elderberrie Translusion Studzies Scholiar, harrumphing notwithstanding. And ofter a beet: — On ultra sail a purée apparatchik comb La Searle rayzone kerbobble duh juiceteafear love Ada dear in sayconned fwaagraa "ma'am shows."

— Exactamung, knotted Waltle Romanarctique sudgaychessly. — Cur "D" any fat, unnerver litterare? Cur communeek tell? Tray purr a key Lacan print. Sir kill ad essential nay paw communicostly own, nay paw enuncyashiki own. La trawdooksy own kipper contra woodrate communicare, knee purée communicare Rianne, daughter cur la communicostly own, dunk kelper shows dinessential. Say la O.C.-land S.&O. kills a raycastersong lay mowvase trawdooksyowns. May sir key dawn unnerver litterare viand ensue dur la communicostly own—eh ma'am? Lure movie trawdookter recon eight rah cur say

3 This is the last sentence in Benjamin's first paragraph and the point at which the translator shifts from translauting homophonically directly from Benjamin's German to working homophonically through Martine Broda's French translation. "Walt the Romantic" is the heteronym to whom this early passage is attributed, presumably because Antoine Berman (2008/2018) argues that Benjamin is a Romantic through and through; but João Ferreira Duarte (1995: 273) and Vivian Liska (2014: 243) argue that these opening salvoes against taking audience response into consideration in studying art is a modernist stance. See DR's *Translation as a Form* (2023f: 16 and 73–75) for discussion.

See the Appendix for all of the source texts, one paragraph at a time, from which DR translauts. [HCE]

loll essential—net ill paw univercellmung recon Newcomb Lindsay sissable, lay posterior, lay "Poway teak"?

— Valuforss,[4] sagd die Art Scholiar.

— Whatever that miens wen 'tis ahome, sneared Waltle Romanoptique. — Sucker lure trawdookter nipper restytour can say pheasant Louis ma'am acrevan? Defray own tush a partear Della on cigoun seen distaunteef della mowvase trawdooksyown, keel A. dunk pairme duh delphinear comb in transmissy own inexact dun countanew innocently yell. Say two jurors lay caw lorecur law trawdooksyown sendgosh a shareveer ler lecture.

— As long, sagd die Art Scholiar, — as the jurors are C.L. and A.

— May C.L. et A. dustynay oh lecture, sagd the Dead Theorist. — Eel foedray cur lore regional O.C. lure few. See, sir! Nepal viscose der Louis keg sistle original, come on purée on day lore comprawned la trawdooksyown a partear daresay rapport?[5]

— Perry vote yeast formal, sagd Walt Romanovtik. — Ross mattress vie aevum cock tacoview, you; me knee up, ha! Deem a vase raw shy 'em, sock a rigging! A Louvre, yum! Zach, loo chin-up! Rahv, lie you, she Perry vote 'em saw cone: Perry Vaw D. Mist!

— Surely not Perry Vaw D. Mist, sagd die Art Scholiar.

— Vaw, prost! cride the Dead Theorist, and they all glinked classes.

— O Perry Vaw D. Mist, O rigging Alya: he may yet divide yucky smeazel! proclamored furrythe r die Art Scholiast. — Own Mozart Oz notch it: nigh dotes alee, valve say sovok—oops, narsty! Cheat tattle lay prize vid any o' ya awe dick Vawt knee Perry vote chick?

— But there's the rub-a-dub, sagd the Dead Theorist. — Eely je, bow lay knee paws reddest Venmo, da puss quietly ah nope hoss vie, eh?

— Sooty Perry vote E., sagd die Art Scholiar. — Tim saw meme v'sought vest V., saws gnaw chee most you. Etty wormy tray boo yet lee? Ah, no, yeah: voe?

4 Along in here Benjamin uses the German verb *gelten*; see Robinson (2023f: 16–18) for a discussion of translating that verb as "has the value/force of." The German verb is actually avoided in this French translation, but apparently the Art Scholar hears its lingering echo. [HCE]

5 And at this juncture the translator finishes translating homophonically from Martine Broda's French translation and begins translauting homophonically from Evgeny Pavlov's Russian translation. Note that in the Russian section "Perry vote" is *perevod* or "translation," "Perry vote chick" is *perevodchik* or "(the) translator," and "Perry Vaw D. Mist" is *perevodimost'* or "translatability." [HCE]
Way to ruin it for everybody, HCE. [DR]
Here *comes* everybody, DR. [HCE]
Ha ha. [DR]

— V. prints hippie, pervy Vaw prost! razed the Dead Theorist this renude tribeaut, and the scholiars all drinked and clank.

— Back to the madder at hen, sagd Walt Romanovchik.

— Aye, agree, sagd the othren.

— Rush Hyatt's a his clue cheat'll no problame nim Putin, sagd Walt Romanovchuk, — Vikroy je oppodick teaches key. Leash Bavarianostomy schlenter, leash aiyai …

— To Roy Vaw prost! enterprupted the Dead Theorist, and they all toted vodka.

— I move that the Dead Theorist remain dead *and silent*, sagd Walt erscottily.

— Secunt! scotted the Dead Theorist.

— All in favor say I.

— I.

— Ai.

— Aye.

— Eye.

— Aye.

— Ai.

— I.

— Loco motion kerries, sagd Walt Romanovsky. — The Dead Theorist will remain mum.

— Whose mum? jorked the Dead Theorist, and chorted richly.

Walt glared. The Dead Theorist quailed and mummed.

— My sample punct, sagd Walt Romanovets, — is that …

— Wate, go baca steppe, sagd a degelate in brichtly colorned costura.

— Hwat now, growned Walt.

— That "Bavarianostomy schlenter," the personne sagd. — You're talking about superficial thinking, methinketh?

— Quitte, sagd Walt.

— In othras paleobras, refereeing to me, the Superficial Thinker, sagd the Superficial Thinker.

— If the shul fist, sagd Walt.

— So what are you saying about me?

— So you'll let me countinue?

— Um galdly.

— My sample punct, restartled Walt Romanovets, — is that Osama Stuy ought'll navels measly ob ya video, Barabbas: nose notch knee me! V'prawn TiVo vest

tacomoo,
pud howdoo,
sledoo,
yet oo,

cause ought stow Opry Deloney, is what I'm trineta say. Yeah, real Yahtzee-ania pun yadda ya sock ran, ya yute Savoy. Yoss snob annoy ya, E., beat mows it, nigh bowl, yeah! Vaginoe snatch chain ya, yes, Lee, that's exonctly richt! Mined if I caul you Lee? (The Superficial Thinker shruggled.) — Premen ya yutes, uh huh, knee toll capo: ought noshin' E.U. k' Jell-O wake you.

— So, sagd the Superficial Thinker, — your sample punct is that we can just entitassily ignomen hunan translouters. Concenter on Bog.

— Not exactionally.

— No, bunt implickiter. You don't want Jell-O to wake you. That's fourcloseting on Jell-O veck, the hummum transluder.

— Capri Maru mojo gov or eat, sagd Walt archily, — O knee zombie vie Amoy she's knee eely knee zombie vie a mom-mom meant yeah, doge

tug da,
cog da,

f'say O neek zombie lee!

Enthusiasmic applouse on all hands, except the dead ones. (And that were all.)

The Superficial Thinker made a dumpokeshow of clapping supersilliantly, roling their eyos.

— I like the part about zombies, they aloud.

— In Russian that part is about forgetting, sagd Walt. — *Zabyli.* Even if every human had forgotten, God would remember.

— Zombie gods, sagd the Superficial Thinker sagdly. — They remember.

— Pleas, inverted the Art Scholiar. — Tell us moro boat the feimed Opry Deloney.

— Ah, amen now, yes, Lee, sagd Walt Romanovtic, glaring the Superficial Thinker into sighlents, — by sloshnest she's knee eely mom meant a knee da puss call a sob veiny, uh, a tot predicate. Ought nude, let me adder, ought nude knee Bilby awshy botch name: own several-nav-several sacklunchal beeb: sib, yeah, tray bovinia, chill a wakem knee vipple, Nemo, yeah. E. Yive Leal saw temps amen silky nah spheroo, g'day anno mudget beet is pole n-no: bomb it bogue, uh? Sot vets Venmo Perry Vaw D. Mist, yes, it's treu, he Covid prize vid indulge naw ASTA Vaught, sir, prayed met 'em. Ross smote Renny, ya dodge a Tom, slew qi, cog da on ninny pud, see Lou, Perry. Vote check 'em vas mojo nostrum chill a wake, uh. Roz veiner? Boo! Deuteronomy, duh.

— Chill a wake, sagd the Superficial Thinker. — That's the Jell-O veck again. The hurmin transbloodletter that we're surposed to cold-should, er.

— But, um, Opry Deloney? noodged the Art Scholiar.

— O yes, Opry Deloney, nocked Walt. — Stephanie Perry! Vaw D. Mimi, yes, Lee, capon yachty you Perry Vaw D. Misty pud I.T. stroganov! Leash-vet Tom—context, yeah (lucking oliver at the Art Scholiar) — sledoo yet Stuy-Veet Vaw prost (*don't even think it, Dead Theorist!*). — Oh, Tom, noodge diet sully v'Perry vodka t' eely-eenier yes he Covid vore Renny, uh. Ibos prove it, Libos, sledoo shoe shay: yes, Lee, Perry vote Yive lie et saw wormy, toe Perry Vaw D. Mist dulls naught nose it's ack sushi nesty Opry Deloney X prize vid any, yeah.[6]

— I.C., sagd the Art Scholiar.

— Rest your vice a wile, sagd Bendix the Kneelplatoonist:[7] — you're hetting goarse.

— I'm find, sagd Waltel Romántico.

— You're knot, sagt Bendix the Kneelplatoonist. — Because the preasing fact is that law Trod Deucey Billy Dodd cone V.N.E. particular minty a seer toss O-bras. Huh? O-bras! Parrow A.O., no key airy de seer K., sue Trod Duke C. own, say a sensy all par a loss O-bras: Ms. Muss see no K.N., sue Trod Duke C., own say many fiesta sierra significaw C.—own in hair rentier hallo rigging all. S. Evvy dente kay Oona Trod Duke C. own, poor bwana kay say a noon cup

6 This is the end of Benjamin's third paragraph, and thus the end of DR translauting Pavlov's Russian. "Opry Deloney," by the way, is nothing earthshakingly important. It's djreamish for *opredelyonyi* "certain," here *opredelyonyi proizvedeniy* "certain works." [HCE]

Next up is the 1971 Spanish translation by Guillermo Alejandro Gómez Alcántara. [HCE]

7 Joyce has "platoonic" (*FW* 348.8); "kneelplatoonist" is presumably "neo-Platonist." See Robinson (2023f: 143–44) for the claim that Benjamin invokes the Jewish neo-Platonism of Philo Judaeus in the "Task." [HCE]

wayday, sig neefy car nod a par a L.O. rigging all; pear O. grassyass ah Sue Trod Deucey Billy Dodd man, T.N.E. Oona real law C. own intimate, cone hell mossy aunt! S. ta

real law C.,
own S.,
taunt O.,
moss S.,
tray cha N.

Law, meh: deed a N.K., par a L.O., rigging all Ms. Mow, ya car essay day significaw C. own!

— A sooner real law C. own kay poo wayday, Cawley fee car say day naw tour all, sagd Dead Wilhelm Dilthey, — E. moss exact a minty, aunt, day V. tall.[8]

— Ah, see, sagt Bendix the Kneelplatoonist with a gnawed ouvert at WD the Dead Hermeneut, — co-molars money fest tossy, honest day law vee da, S. tawn in team a minty. Real law, see, O nadas

cone toe dough,
sare vee voe,
a honky no,

representin' nada par a S. day (Tom bein' law Trod Duke C. own bro). Ta dell O. rigging, all pair oh no, taunt oh day, sue vee da comb O. day, sue "super V. Vincy ah" poo-ace! Law Trod Duke C., own ace posterior all O. rigging all. E. scene embargo, par a loss O-bras import aunties, key noon caw en Gwen tron, ah. Sues Trod Duke Tories

8 This is translauted from Gómez Alcántara's truncation of Benjamin's important allusion to Wilhelm Dilthey: "Er darf ein natürlicher genannt werden und zwar genauer ein Zusammenhang des Lebens" (1923/1972: 10), "It may be called 'natural' and indeed an intertwining of life"; Gómez Alcántara makes it "Es una relación que puede calificarse de natural y, más exactamente aun, de vital," "It is a relation that can be qualified as natural and, even more exactly, as vital" (like life). Dilthey's *Zusammenhang des Lebens* "nexus/intertwining of life" becomes a "vital relation." See Robinson (2023f: 39–41) for a fuller explanation.

In this Spanish paragraph "Trod Duke Tories" are *traductores* "translators," "Trod Duke C. own" is *traducción* "translation" and "Trod Deucey Billy Dodd" is *traducibilidad* "translatability." [HCE]

avocados en la A. Poe caw day, sue cray ah C. own in dick a law fa zeta day, sue super V. Vincy ah, law E. day ah day law

V.-daw
E.-day.

Law super V. Vincy ah day loss O-bras, Debby N10! Dare say Conan rigor toe tall minty ex sent oh day meh ta for us.

— Shouldern't that be E.A. Poe? queeried the Art Scholiar.

— No, sagd Bendix the Kneelplatoonist, — it's "A. Poe caw," from *época*, "epoch." It's not Edgar Allen Poe come back to quasilife in this djream.

— Quasilife as the afterlife? fullered up the Art Scholiar. — Isn't that what "super V. Vincy ah" is trying to get at?

— "Afterlife," sagd Bendix the Kneelplatoonist, — is howl Harry Zohn and Steven Rendall translouted Benjamin's *Überleben*, hwich is litteraminimally "superlife" or "overlife." The Circe text don't die and it don't come back to no life; it's supersizzled. Gómez Alcántara's *supervivencia* is "survival," metamorphologically "superexperience" or "overexperience": much closer than Zohn and Rendall.

— But, sagd the Superficial Thinker: — the work of art is *alive*? We have to understand that as "totally exempt from metaphors"?

— Well, sagd Bendix the Kneelplatoonist, — knee Siggy era en las A. Poe caw's day, my yore cone foo C. own men tall say, ah, soup west, okay? Solo el organ east mow pooty era, a star dough-ta-dough day V.-da.

— So, hwat, sagd the Superficial Thinker, — "not even in times of greatest mental confusion has it been supposed that only the *organism* could be endowed with life"? By "organismo" Goméz Alcántara means what you call *die organische Leiblichkeit*, "organic corporeality"?

— Aye.

— So, what ayere we tonking avout? That Graunde Dame Alma, the Soul?

— No, sagd Bendix the Kneelplatoonist: — A.O. no ace rawzone,

par a pray 10,
dare ex 10,
dare el impair E.O.,
day law V.-da
bah ho,

el fra heel set row dell Alma, comb oh low intent oh Fechner, but that's opposurd.

— So, what then, sensation?

— Of coarsair not, sagd Bendix the Kneelplatoonist: — ne Tom Poe co par a day, sere key Sharia Poe see blay, deaf fee near law vV.-da bossanddough, say en lows octos toedavia. Maynose dayC.C.voes, day law any Molly Dodd, O.N.L. sent teamy into, K. solo law carrack Teresa O. cause C. ownallminty.

— Good old Molly Dodd and her brother Billy, sagd the Superficial Thinker. — Molly always was all minty. She and C.C.

— Veiry phunny.

— So, sagd the Superficial Thinker: — boddilies are charlatacterized by senseishun *only occasiolly*? Sommetimes yes, summertimes no?

— S.-tay coneseptic, say, who's teefycaw? queeried Wally the Histaminorian. — May whore quantdough, say, atreebooyah a K.O.K., ah H.O., ease Tory, ah; E. no uh see dough?

— I gette the "ease Tory, ah," sagd the Superficial Thinker: — that's history, which of coarse is alloways "his" and "Tory." But hwoo is the *May whore quant* and hwat do she do?

— Ooh, kneecawminty S.N.R.E.O., day A., ya! sagd Wally the Histamajorian. — Pork K.N. owl team, O tareminnow solo poowayday, daytare mean arsay el armbeatoh day law, V.-da! Livin it! Livin it low, caw! Partyendough day la easeTorya E., no day law gnaw tirra lezzy, E. mucho menusee day cozies, tawn vorryoblays, comb O! L. sent teamy N. toe E.L., Alma Day! Aye, Alma Day! A.E.K. corres-pond a-all, phillosofaux law, missyown day intairp ray tart owe da law V.-da nawtourall, party N. dough, day law ex—sis—ten—see—a moss amply a day law is Tory a E.N., toe dough caws O, law super V. Vincyah day las O-bras, no S. income parablay minty moss, fossil day raycone O sare kay law day loss creeatourass? Law is Tory a day, loss groandays O-bras,

day are
tay are
on caw
day lows

oh ree hennas,

day law
V.-daw,

say a fourmotto dour auntie law V.-da, law-D.-da, dell are teased ta E., loss henera C. owness owl tare E.O. rays sone S.N.C. allminty loss kay lay conefeeerrand,

ooh, naw,
super V. Vincy ah
do rah dare rah.

— Quant oh say money fiesta-esta super V. Vincy ah, sagd die Art Scholiar, — that dourable superliffey, toema L. Noam bray day pharma.

— It drinks the name? e-quipt the Superficial Thinker. — Let's drink to the fame!

They drink the vodka and name the fame. All except the Dead Theorist, who find their lips myshteariantly sealed.

— Loss Trod Duke C. own ace kay sone "I'll go," sagd Bendix the Kneelplatoonist, — moss kay comb Mooney, caw C. own ace sewer, hen quant oh Oona O-bra,

sew bray,
V. vey,
E. Arkansas law A.,
Poe caw day,

sue pharma. Poor cone see Ghent A., loss Trod Duke C. own ace, no sone loss kay press tawn unser vee,

see O.,
à la O-bra,
comb O.

Pretendin' lows mallows Trod Duke Tories, see no kay moss bein' Deb N., ah law O-bra sue ex-sis10, see? ahh. Law V.-da dell O. rigging all Arkansas N.A.S., sue ex-ponzi own posthuma mouse, vaster ah E.C.M., pray rain Nevada![9]

9 This is the last sentence of the translauting from Spanish; next DR translauts from the 2005 Chinese translation by Chen Yongguo. In this section "fanny" is *fānyì* or 翻译 "translate, translation."

Caveat emptor, though: in a book review a few years ago a rather irascible Sinologist warned readers never to trust anything DR says or writes about Chinese. [HCE]

Including that caveat in the previous paragraph. [DR]

— Ya Joan t' shooed uh-huh?—gougey duh?, sagd Wilhelm Dilthey. — Humming sing, sure, de junky go chum-ya showdown ye Joan t' shooed uh, gougey de moody sing soljer way. Slung mean you, moody singjer Jen de g'wan, see? Consumming seein' Ron, are gee who chow wager leader John, whoa, jer yodeseye slung mean de so-yo grr bee a moody sing so chew song-de Joan gee moody-boo shurdseye cheesy shundling you are shurdseye gunggowda ling you leadery taw-n-tao shirtseye seein' shirtsy shun. Slung mean de ye chiamoo de Sing-Sing, sure, bow cool cheesy shunned a moody sing, g'way gun Gia D., boodseye, you slung mean, hardseye, you slung mean bunjer dubyow, doddseye, you cheehoney deadseye seein'!

— What's that about *guanxi*, Billy Budd? sagd the Elderskerry Transloxin Stunts Sculler. — That there's a bribe, if I'm not mistackled. Ain't sure that's appriaprate …

— Holed yer holsters, there, E.T.S.S., sagd Bendix the Kneelplatoonist. — I believe brimebury is but one whey of mainlining a *relationship*, hwich is the hire-order umberella turm sigglefied in Qina by *guanxi*. In fact, Herr Dilthey, wooden shoe guest that *guanxi* was Mr. Chen's Qinese translation of your *Zusammenhang*? The *intertwining* of life, which is to say slung mean or shengming, and of purposiveness, which is to say moody, *mùdì*, 目的.

— I hate to see a purposiveness go all moody like that, quippled the Superficial Thinker.

— Yincy fannysway Johnnyway manzoo, whoa! sagd Schönflies the Crabblist, spilking up for the furst dime. — Mend a sooyow, are da dowbyow C&U engines neighboo g'wan see de moody? Taboo cur numb, gee, sure, ho, chewy leejer Joanie insane de g'wan see bunshun, dawn chewy curry tong goopy tie de ho John hoo-waahed ba sing sure-sure seein' jer Joan g'wan see are John cheedseye seein'. Sure twoedseye, pay to tie Joan Jett ye chewy leader tonsure yejer mowsure woo!

— "Pay to tie Joan Jett"? sagd the Elderly Transolution Standees Scroller, aghost. — Some sortov bondrage grame?

— It's a homopheronic transmultation from the Chinglese, you old fartfarther, sagd Walt. — It's 试图在胚胎中加以 *shìtú zài pēitāi zhōng jiāyǐ*, literamully "try in embroglyo middle to add." 胚胎 *pēitāi*, embroglyo. Imbrogno. Indryo.

— But that's no bettor, sagd the Elder. — Genemetic imagenjeering!?

— Nod a humean embrondlyo, sagd Benjy the Exhorticulturalist. — A plant embrondlyo. A germun. In Germun *ein Keim*.

— Since hwen do you know Chinglese, germumbled the elder embrondlyonically to Walt. — And Germun, he tried to Benjy middle to add.

— It's anxtually an adverbantial colaustrio there, sagd Walt, — like "embroglyonically." To make it reyal embroglyonically or intrensivately. *Indem sie es* ***keimhaft*** *oder intensiv verwirklicht.*

— D'wager Joan sure woodedseye seein' Jew yo rootsy do t' de singjer, cölntinwed Walt Romaunce the Tick. — Yejer you'd'seye fay you yen shun ho lynching gee shall zowl de dow. Zilchey labia sang jung Joan, ta curry Eli cheata fangsure and sure E.E., are fay John hoo-waahed a—gee, you, Jen, singed a ansured a—sure thing.

— Talk about hoo-waa, sagd the Superficial Thinker.

— And sorry agin but what's all this talk about that chewy leejer-ho Joan Jett and her zilchey labia, and Johnny and his yincy bunshun fannysway? sagd the Elderhostile Transfusion Stodgies Scholiast. — My years are burning.

— I believe, sagd Bendix the Kneelplatoonist, that Schönflies our devaunted Crabblist was puncting us towoods "you, Jen, singed a" namely *yùjiàn xìng de* or 预见性的, "prophetic."

— Thank you, sagd Schönflies the Crabblist, with a bonhomous bao Bendixwarf. — Jer you jotting de you engine, de needs I chin you and sing? Ze E.E. Joan

t' shoo
d' choo

tonguesing way byowjer. Jer Joan t' shoo de chin you on; sing sure, John, John de Jew jow-de, inveigh grr! Joan, you yen Jewy boosure sang who mow slung-de, are sure seein' yen D., chew luh so yo leisure, g'wan: see? Jer why hardseye tommin' so beyowda de dongsee shangsang who gone leyonda?[10]

— Aha! sagd the Elderfuthark Transolution Sturdies Scholaris. — Damn silly tissy, write us naughty, seek out inking, pal! Out tavern sarkast elongate our peotomy 'n clear to tadin' yell-cane talk-guys in parenting canners Tay Yuri Ann. You'se canners' 10 datavanna on

10 This is the end of DR's translaut from Chen's Chinese translation. Next he translauts from the Finnish translation by his old (now dead) friend Leevi Lehto, in which "canners" is *käännös* "translation," "canner-kisser" is *käännöksissä* "in translations," "contamining" is *kääntäminen* "translating," and "cantayeah" is *kääntäjä* "translator." [HCE]

toadies' tackle 10 seaside t' sue cooleye pseuda, me 10 mootornado civet SIDA sorry you too aucune valid Amalfi modelist simmin' sarcastial cootie oxen moo-down Yahtzee salon?

— Pshaw, sagd Bendeix the Kneelplatoonist. — My needy tea Orient A. cute&gone, Ollie cue¬e tackyman, sicko damnin' dark couldn't cast east of acre neen, moodown barium alternose sodaman meek a cannerkisser on olé lister. Do-si-dossy-ace a kill 10 sue cooleye Seuss, ill mannikin cannerkisser ballson souvenir ya Tasmania's amencuing cotton ruin, a whaleman penally sinner! Ya meh Ritalin mattermanner shaman lies Utena.

— All cute oxen ya cannerxen towed Ellis, sagd the Psiologist. — In sudden immaterial sexy wormy turfvow to argument teen, yoga car yell 10 thousand vast a teadown Cree teakisser Hayashi day Oreo mod Otto mood innocent Amish sexy cow teats to ya-ya two-school cool ya. Cootin' alky my cessahose soy-tit on Edda teadown objectivy sluice ya cell liaison perky meanin' keen O Lisi ma doughtone ta, you'se damn American younkers towed Ellis in hey just doomaxe wormy dazzle vitaminetta you'se canners' old musky Elton Tatarsy someone called isotanal cutey oxen cons a contamining A. ewly bristal O Lisi ma doughlister.

— All cute oxen eh lammin', sagd Bendeix the Kneelplatoonist. — Yacht comin' in neen coin itsy sauna keeno sorta mare keepsake geeminy time: Seine lock-a-motto Tommy-tummy stay UDIs (tummy stay). Low policing Atkin saw none valleynut mood duvet ya coop civet ate a lane I yawn my ota. Yo keen

me cah
I can naan
A. cah
O leevine!

Idyll on olive amah dolly, Seuss: ruin oilyawn kill a Savoy mirrorhemming

coolhost a
coolluna realty a

tiatoot saunavalleynut voivode sittin' sottaw Lee Kelly, keelin' immanent

teyya
tendon
seyya;

yolkin' aichernaan two or rail tattooin' doughnut void; mirrorhemming cool host a cool luna realty a aichernaan yoga pievine in viecutter archiveseldom.

— That's all find and gone, sagd the Psichronogist. — But Tallahassee moodtoastin' coin merce ophthalaila lockcalmatom Ian marekey Tissier tomb, Ian olé!

moxie 'n hockey meanin',
yellkey poleveein',
subjectivitastytas killin',
ya killyloomin',
eh lammin',

see rasta mare key tsetse, yo: allcail eachseemin' keen, sicko low gismo invalotsa pyetse soon ya swearoxen sackoy Tom Mista Merce, ya annan, mood a soonatom Ian yadda vaticman Heidel

(m)alice10 history
Alice10 process

Ian seaview Tom Mista Silicon hankie-san liescootin voxy. Yavapai caw gearyeye Lilian V. Maine in kerningwidow, joshcuss onustootteasingking, O sodaman handin' tuxysenza, cool a monkeyvexy damnhackin'! A.V.L.A. palacedicey kissy stackolewdster canners tayloria.

— Stay that agrein? sagd the Superficial Thinker.

— Hwich part? sagd the Slychologrist. — Stackolewdster canners tayloria?

— The veri same, sagd the Superficial Thinker. — Ain't that about the "dead theory of translation"?

— Mm-mm! sagd the Dead Theorist.

— *Kyseistä kuollutta käännösteoriaa*, sagd the Superficial Thinker.

— Mm-mm! sagd the Dead Theorist.

— Ainchew gone let the poor fella talk about it? sagd the Superficial Thinker to Valtteri Romantikko. — Jusk for a mini-minit?

The Dead Theorist mummed and dummed.

The Dead Theorist riggletto and giggletto.

Walt Romantikko glaired. Then repented and relented.

A handwaive.

— Thank you, sagd the Dead Theorist. — A translotion is a textus laid out on the table nextus annoither textus. Aye, laid out, to faxilipate scienterrific cumpairison.

— A translation is *not* a dead thing that can be laid out on a table for vividsexion, sagd Bendix the Kneelplatoonist. You just want to make everything as dead as you are.

— Yer dead two, sagd the Dead Theorist. — We're all dead. Somebody is djreaming us back into quasixistence, where we can talk but not make much sense. You least of all, Kneelcartoonist.

— Platoonist! cride Bendix the Kneelplatoonist.

— Same differmince, sagd the Dead Theorist.

— Translavation, sagd Bendix the Kneelplatoonist, — is a leaving arganism that grose and changes oever time. After ill, silly neen coin certain ruined oilmen salvoed yessy salad vocisadden sawtoaster mooduvet toucanon toyseeks neen mood too merce cantayeah Edenkilly. Neen on ooppaymanking cannerxen Osama ophtha eyecah onta pawnoxen saw Oman killin' saw cosviewin' ya louwheeze towards Seine moodaccess saw. Neen cowass canners yeah tuya stasis ah modestica den colane killin' Valium eta guy kissed a tidymodesty Urizen oh-so-soxy low-key owlsooty neen viarighten Samoyed yellkeytoolanetomistah coin ohmien poltergeists.[11]

— And "colane killin'" there, sagt the Dead Theorist, — is "dead language." The punct is that transvaluation is no daub eitchoing of one dead language in anothrum. In facit of all limperary vorms it is the one encrusted with two crimptical tashkes: trashking both the changes in the sirce language in the coarce text's ofter-ripensis and the target tong's barth pangs in the oridginal's transloffal superleaf.

4b

The Study Session (the text-plus-annotations of the kids studying upstairs in *FW* Chapter II.2[12]).

The seen changelings. The odditorium fagues away. A long oakum werkatable emergers. Our degellans sit alongst it, pouring over vellumstrated manuscrimp painges, scribbling annodominations. The room appears to be a medieval scriptorium. The text is …

11 This is the end of the translauting from Leevi Lehto's Finnish translation. The one last remaining paragraph of section 4a is a portmanteauskewing of Benjamin's German. [HCE]

12 II.2 is the *FW* chapter from which the "translout that gaswind into turfish" line was taken and discussed in the Preface. One surmises that the change is nothing more mysterious than DR running out of languages they can play nicely with. [HCE]
Let's see you do better. [DR]

The kinnedschipp betwixt any two lengargles is not hystorical but souprahystorical (the hystery of supperlief), and consistorias not in the kinder structional similanity traditorially explorded in counterastive lingogistics, but in the fract that the same (no)thing is mentaled in neach, namilly that hwich can be antrained by no singumar one of them on its own, but only by the karllectanity of their murchally soupplemintyd sinterentions: peeure langolidge. But in their urntentiousnesses langolidges soupplemynt each other. This is one of the most fondermental loss in the philanthroposophy of longuarge. To grasimp it foolly, one must distilanguish between hwat is nintended (the *interndendumb*) and the männör in hwich it is hintrended. In the Guerman and Franch words for "bread," *Brot* and *pain*, hwat is "meunt" or "skintendered" (the *intradendritus*) is the same;[13] but in the modeus siggonyfeecandy they mane different dings to Chermans and the Fronch, so they are not mulchually inkschangeable; their yoursage tendoncies in the twa lenguahis are twowoard moochial inksclosion. In an absdolute since, however, in turms of the *intrendardum*, they meme exactomtitly the seam thing. Wile the mowedhis signiffycando is in comflickt in the tvo vords, the

Bendix the Kneelplatoonist (BKP): Pure language! That's what I'm talking about.
Duns Scotus (DS): He means what I called the *modus significandi*.
ETSS: Give me an example.
Schönflies the Crabblist (SC):
He's hinting here at Lurianic Crabblism: the clash of languages, the rubbing against each

Elderly TS Scholar (ETSS): Obviously all the individual elements in two languages are mutually exclusive. There is no reason to think that these would ever match up in a translation.

Superficial Thinker (ST): I see that WB is discussing

13 What, Jesus's flesh? [ETSS]
Certainly not! [BKP]
But the *intendendum* of *pain* in Baudelaire and *Brot* in your translouchal of Baudelaire is the Eucharist bread. That's what unites those two words. [ETSS]
My thought is grounded in the Jewish Kneelplatoonism of Philo Judaeus, *before* that false prophet Jesus. [BKP]
Keep telling yourself that. [ETSS]
See Robinson and Sun (2025) for more fun with Baudelaire. [HCE]

other, is all the Crabblist e-scatological prediction.

SC: Wrapped in those *kelipot* shells of evil.
BKP: For Philo the Jewish Messiah was the Logos, a Demiurgic mediator between God and humans.

Benjy the Exhorticulturist (BE): Sacred history as plant, from seed to stalk to kernel.

conflectuating maniers of inelevending also enemter into a reloution of motrill supplicantation in the two spreakens. And in dreed in this case the männör of intendencing entrees into a relusion of muchlial sumplemictation with the *intendendum*. In eitch individeold (ansupplemintyd) tongway we nerver feind hwat is intrended in relaytivo indiaprendence, in invidivual vords or sentimences; rother, it is constandingly churbling and changling, until it manacles to remerge from the hardemony of all the intendive womanners as puerile languorge. Untarl then it remands hiddled in the linguiges. But if the lenguajeeps keep growling like this until the messyanic endit of their hystery, the eturnal angoling laif of littermary wirks and the undendring ooflayben of langanges enkringle transolution to keep prouving the wholy groath of languages, testicking how far removered what is sestraquestered inside them is from relevation, and how pressentive it might become thrue nolidge of the removeral.

But hunan transloation is only a hitlormist way of distoloving the fernness of furren langoges: the hability to distolove the probuslem of that furriness instanter or concludantly is denayled to hummins, or at least cannot be sotted immedicartably. The necrossary medicartability can be found in the glowth of religiamaroles, which ripellens the seamen that is hiddled in the languages and razes it to a hihear liveau. Unlick ars, transalacion can neveren lei clame to the longandurance of its prodigts, but it steel kips striveting to glane a last delfinirv stamadge of languic providustence. In a tranxilation the sowrath

the mystical messianism that SC likes so much over in the left margin, and I should really be suspicious and resistant, but I kind of like the feignomenology of the"churbling and changling" of source & target languages.

SC: But for Lewrianal Crabblism what is "sestraquestered" is the reunification of the Ein Sof.
ST: "Sestra-what?" Someone's Russian sister?

BE: Seed as seamen; the growth of religions as the glowth of rigamaroles!

The "colonel" is the kernel (the edible part of a nut, the stone of a peach or plum, or the seed or grain of corn). *SC*: The seed or kernel is hidden in the fruit as the divine life of pure language is hidden in a text or a language is hidden. The outer covering is the kelipot shell that must be rubbed off.

ETSS: BKP and SC and the others are describing translation in general, not *this* translouting. Ignore that long series of unserious questions posed by ST in the right-hand margin.

textle grose into a heigher and puerer realem of llenguatge—and even thole it can't leave there forestever, because it neer artaints that realimb in evary expect, it still punts in a wunderbar hantée wée toowoord the predestrianed yet inassecsible cuningdom of langueric rectonsilliation and filfullament. Thru transtilation the origgingle does not rache that umpire strumpandstrile, but it does crumbtain that inspect of the transtitilation that does not transvet a messyge. More preciopiticely, that aspential essect is the colonel of un(re) transloutability in any transloution. The meening or spince of any text can indeed be translouted; but no mander how much of it the translouter sikhs to extruct from the oridgismal and transpit in the translortion, this gaffort will lave untorched the elemint woward hwich the treu translantor's wirk is stirped. Like the aroginal's poet-word, that elemint is untranslootable, bycause the rellasion betwaxt the tender and the limba[14] is differmint in the orienginal and the transliquefaction. In the oleoginal, teneur and langue are jerned togather with a sartain youknitty, like a frutte and its skind, whyle in the translution the lingwa is wrappéed loosemically around the tenzer, like the uuide pleasing pliis of a roynal womantle. For a transelation ponts to a kaliba[15] heugher than its own, and as a rensult remanits at violate auds with and aliadulterated from its own tenord. This rupliture rendifies the transrendition itself transunrendible, and at the same time makes it supererotigant. For every transolution

ST: Does *this* translation of the "Aufgabe" represent all other translations into all other languages? What *is* this rejoycing translation's target language at this specific point in history?

14 *Limba* is Romanian for "language." You'll probably guess that *lingwa* means "language" too, a few lines down, but may not guess that it's actually the Maltese word for it. [HCE]

15 *Kalba* is Lithuanian for "language." [HCE]

ETSS: Wait, what, WR? The Romantics didn't think much about translation? They were more interested in criticism?

of a weirk at a specificate puncture in the herstery of the sprooch[16] reprenders, with regartta to a gefane shore of its tenore, transolution into all other sprooches. Ironiserly ain'tshe[17] iwwersetting iwwerplants the origenial into a more entertailechial royalm of language, out of hwich it cannot be movered by a nieuw transcolligation; it can only be eleventhated to it oberandober and in other instandings. It is no coincerence that the paleobra "ironiserly" remainds us of the Romanticos, with their nonpaderailed innersleight into the liffe of arswyrks, to witch'n'tug hurry isuzu[18] attestes most eloquatically. Of geese the Romanticos didn't quite desturminate transtugation as an attestimany of that swort; they were much more intertested in criticalithumpism, hwich also playas its (more trivisel) rolle in the evoluent liefe of the wirking of litorature. But even

What is the "gefane shore of its tenore"? Does it have just one tenor? Perhaps it sings in disharmony with a largemouth bass, an alto coffee, and Tony Soprano? Does it have just one shore? Does it have just one type of shore? Is one of them the Comedy Store serially owned and run by Sammy, Mitzi, and Pauly Shore?

16 *Sprooch* is Luxembourgish for "language," and *iwwersetzung* a few lines down is Luxembourgish for "translation." [HCE]

17 Sweet! [DT]

18 Just curious, HCE: what's a "witch'n'tug hurry isuzu"? [ST]
Ntụgharị asụsụ is Igbo for a translation (the witch is just "which"). "To translate" is *sụgharịa*. [HCE]

Walt the Romantico (WR): Well, it's true. Sure, they wrote a few aphorisms about translation, but nothing of any weight.
ETSS: Look out, ST, WR's stealing your superficial thunder here.
WR: That's not fair.

thow they wackytoon wended their theowrising werger-ward at all, the wyld wyrk they wardled as wergerandins was windfarmed by a warmfeel for the wayzin and worth of trainswaystation as a forworm.[19] All winksnhints are that the Wromantreacle warmfeel for the wheezin and werth of wertling as a wohorm need not be wiggerest in the worsefier; in thwact the powwowit may have the weekissed wuum for it. The wontoned witsdum is that ponetors make the best transponetors and a medievochre poletor will be a medievochre transpoletor; but hystyry does not even once subport that. A whoale ryeow of the grossetest Germaniacal wriders, zoom by shpiel Luther, Voß, and Schlegel, are inmaysurawbbly waydjur as transtonors than as poecats, n'othiers, inkludering Hölderlin und George, kanrot justasfriably be echlaimed as poenuts allone if the foal bathyscope of their shutput, in partyquler their work as 40toes,[20] is brokurd into considination. Alftorall, 4dit is a 4m in its ohmrite, so 2 is the 2x20toe's taxits ohm4m, which muisty dustinglished from that of the Poe8.

ST: Hey, cut him some slack, ETSS! I'm sitting here lolling in admiration for all the wuh-wuhs along through here. Freddy Slier-maker never wrote about "the wyld wyrk they wardled as wergerandins was wind-farmed by a warmfeel for the wayzin and worth of trans-waystation as a forworm."

19 What's a wergerandin, then? [WR]
Kurdish for a translator. And *werger* is Kurdish for a translation. And "wackytoon" seems to be *wekî tune*, Kurdish for "hardly at all." [HCE]
Kurdish? Why on earth? [WR]
Who cares? It's beautiful! [ST]

20 I assume "40toke" hints at *fortitók*, Hungarian for "translators." "4dit" in the next line would be *fordít* "translation." [HCE]
Do we really need numbers here? [ST]
What would Joyce do? (ETSS)

ETSS: If you had only *mentioned* Fred Slidermayor's 1813 Academy address, shown you had even *heard* of it …

The icetreethor's[21] tasc involutes feinding that intenhut in the 2-yehzeek[22] that awachens the yecchoe of the oremidginal's frump-yahziik. This is an aspitch of porktheemie[23] that radishly distantwishes it from the wark of the pawit, whose in10hut is naver trenned on the sprog[24] as such, on its todality, but ownly immediabloy on spacifick tanner-inteatuinings. But unlike the litterarely ouregonal, hwich pennetraits depp into the soreskeel's[25] innair moontin fourest, the trans*e*lation stands offside[26] the weold and kawls into it withinorout oever stetting fuss in it, sweeking that one sweek swot where the swisslimba ewcho will rewerb the swistixt in the twotong.

21 "Icetreethor" hints as *aistritheoir*, Irish for "translator." [HCE]
22 "Yehzeek" and "yahziik" as *jezik*, Bosnian for language? 2 for "to," as in "toward," as in "target language"? [HCE]
23 HCE, do we have a gloss on "porktheemie"? [ETSS]
"Translation" in Albanian (*përkthimi*). [HCE]
24 *Sprog* is Danish for "language." [HCE]
25 "Sores" seems to hint at "source," and *keel* is Estonian for "language," hence "soreskeel" would be "source language." [HCE]
Of course a skeel is a shallow wooden vessel or washtub in Scotland, and got used for a two-handled bucket (FI *haarikka*) in my translation of Aleksis Kivi's *The Brothers Seven.* Just sayin. [DR]
Hard to imagine that skeel feeling sore, though. [ST]
26 Offside? Sideswipe? Pinstripe? [DT]

ST: What's this?
A pome?[27]
BE: Or the echo of a pome, from outside the apple orchard?

BKP:
Have you heard of Translation's Intention
How 'twas travin'd 'pon somebitten other
(Chorus) Than that of the pome
Than that of the pome?
Frukt!
Namely 'twas travin'd upon a long ludic langwidge
A lungwidge, la, taken (or token) 'nits toadamity
(Chorus) The best kind of toad
The best kind of amity
Cal-*amity!*
Hetero-*gamity!*
Insweeted it was, aye, through a swingle artwork
(Chorus) In a foreign toung
The tang of a furring yonge
The tingle upon its tongle
Daring!
But 'tis in itswelf iwis other, or awthor
(Chorus) The ibis-bit frother
The ox-tailed rother
Do!

ST: The apple was sweet, but felt furring on the tongue.

ETSS: And who's this Chorus?

ST: Chorus of in-anity?
DT: Sean & Seamus Hav-anity?
ST: O. Hugh Mannity …

27 Cf. *Finnegans Wake* pp. 45–47. [HCE]

The poet's nintendion is nigheve, a colorful leedre
The translator's is guydead, a mindfield follower
(Chorus) Not mindless no never
Not a guyder no never
Fie! Fife!

WR: Isn't a *forss* a rapids in Swedish?
ST: Take it away, Schöenflies the Crabblist!

For the gross moltivating forss
Of the blintegration
Of many languidges into One True One
Is on the jobb.
(Chorus) *Pure Jenkki!*[28]

SC:
That (dis)integrative farce, howsome'air, is the one
In hwich individual sendunces,
Lines of werse &
Juggerments ne'er correspond,

WR: "Pure language" is no messianic apocalypse; it's a game of Jenga played orally, in dialect(ic). It's Fred Hurldarlin pulling a wooden block out of his tottering tower.[29]

28 This is a bilingual joke in Finnish and English. Jenkki is a Finnish chewing gum; the name means "Yankee," so in English the advertising slogan "Pure Jenkki" (originally spoken in the TV commercials by Bob Grant from *On the Buses*—not a Yankee TV show) means "pure American." But *pure* in Finnish is also the imperative form of the verb for "bite" and "chew," hence "chew our gum," but also "bite an American." [HCE]

29 Antoine Berman (2008/2018: 129), as translated by Chantal Wright: "But Benjamin's *rein* has an additional source: Hölderlin, whose poetic language is governed by *Reinheit*, by purity (although the poet could also have borrowed this from Kant whom he viewed as the 'Moses' of the German nation). *Rein*, for Hölderlin, is what connects us to the source. We have to be attentive to the echo, in Benjamin, of this Hölderlinian *rein*, which is felt in many of his poems in the sense I have indicated above. Poetic language—to the extent that poetry becomes language—is pure language, language which is 'pure song'. Benjamin's Messianic announcement of 'pure language' might secretly correspond to Hölderlin's prophetic *Bald sind wir Gesang* [Soon we shall be song]." [HCE]

For they remain at the beckoncall of transolation.
(Chorus) But in that True Language
The zebret languages
Of hiwch it is compromised
Miuchally supplemintyd
& wreckonciled *('ciled, 'ciled)*
In the modusties of their indentation
Lacross o'er into younison.
(yes they)
Lacross o'er into younison.[30]
But if there trooly is a llangwage of trooth
And in that llangwage of trooth
(Chorus) Without sudspinse
Or even the spocken pollabra
If in that …

DT: Does "zebret" mean the languages have vertical black and white stripes?

ST: A big "if."
DT: Suspense as the sud spin cycle on your washing machine.

Berman also ties Benjamin's *reine Sprache* to Kant's *reine Vernunft* ("pure reason"), noting that for Kant *das Reine* "the pure" is "everything that is *a priori* in nature: the pure forms of intuition, the categories of understanding, the concepts of reason" (129). [DR]
Stand down, DR. I got this. [HCE]
Yeah but— [DR]
—But how many wooden blocks? [DT]

30 "You" in English and 你 "ni" in Chinese both refer to the same second person ("younison" as your son?). [ETSS] "Unison" as a mode of singing. *Bald sind wir Gesang*. [WR]

The alltimete mystories that all thocht labbers to revele
(Chorus) are klept
are klept
Then

ST: "The ultimate mysteries that all thought labors to reveal" rejoyced into lab technicians reveling in my stories from all time. Uh huh.

ST: I want a sandy sprog! I don't care if the author's reasoning is circular!

Then that sprog of sandhead[31] is the sandy sprog
A-and! the only perphexion pherloxophers
can e'er houpe to achouve
Is to divyne and discryde that sprog
That's internsively congealed in tradookoy[32]

BE: No mashed potatoes, no phyllo pastries, and—no Sufis?—at this toga party?

There is no muusi[33] of phyllosuufi
and

31 *Sprog* is Danish for "language" and *sandhed* is Danish for "truth"; "language of truth" would be *sandhedens sprog*. [HCE]

32 *Tradukoj* is Esperanto for "translations." [HCE]
In English of course "dookie" is a bathing suit (Scotland), a Baptist (UK), or feces (US). Add "trans-" to each of those and see what you get. [DT]

33 *Muusi* is Finnish for "mash" (cognate of English "mush," derived from Swedish *mos* "mash," pronounced "moose"). The Finnish for "muse" would be *muusa*. [HCE]

WR: The work itselpinna[34] does is less marked than both, but the mark it leaves on history is etched just as deep.	There ain't one of no tolgaparty[35] neither But that don't mean *(No matter what them* *Maudlin artists'll tell ya)*
ST: Both what? *WR*: Poetic creation and teaching. Pay attention.	That phyllosuufi and umberharvestus[36] be ba-ba-bop … (Chorus) *Banausic*! Ba-ba-bop … (Chorus) *Banausic*! *Banausic*!

34 "Itselpinna" seems to hint at *itzulpena*, Basque for "translation." "Hiscuntsa" over in the right margin also seems to be Basque: *hizkuntza* is "language." [HCE]
I don't like to see that kind of coarse language in a serious academic treatise. [ETSS]
Be that as it may, for some reason "chorus" in this French poem is written in Basque (*koru*). [HCE]
Oh, I thought that was the Finnish for a piece of jewelry—? [DR]

35 "Tolgaparty" seems to combine the Estonian for "translation" (*tõlge*) with the Russian name Olga and the English togaparty. [HCE]

36 *Ümberarvestus* is another Estonian word for "translation," but in the broad sense of restating, recounting, reappraising. [HCE]
Based on Finnish I would guess that *ümberarvestus* (FI **ympäriarvostus*) is morphologically a reappraisal first and a translation second. [DR]
Look, what did I ask you? Hm? [HCE]
No, you look. Who told you to start annotating foreign words for "translation" and "language"? Did James Joyce do that in *Finnegans Wake*? Ever? You're the one spoiling the purity of the Joyce imitation. [DR]
"Purity"? You're starting to sound like BKP and SC. [HCE]
Well you don't sound a bit like Humphrey Chimpden Earwicker. [DR]
I'm Here Comes Everybody. [HCE]

There is a jeanyus philosophickal that is poessessed
(Chorus) of a yarning for that idioomi
that is manifestoed in translatsiooni

ST: I can't read French. Could someone please translout that gaswind into turfish?[37]

Stéphane Mallarmé (S&M):
Les langues imparfaites en
(Koru) cela que plusieurs,
manque la suprême:
penser étant écrire sans accessoires,
(Koru) ni chuchotement
mais tacite encore l'immortelle parole,
(Koru) la diversité,
sur terre,
des idiomes empêche personne de proférer
(Koru) les mots qui,
sinon se trouveraient,
par une frappe unique,
elle-même matériellement la vérité.

WR: If S&M isn't blowing smoke here, itselpinna (with that germ of hiscuntsa that speaks that truth) stuns midway between poetic creation and teaching.

37 "Languages, imperfect in their plurality, lack the supreme thing: thinking being writing without accessories, without even whispers, the immortal word is still unspoken; the diversity of languages on earth makes it impossible to speak the words that would otherwise, in a single stroke, assume material form as truth." [HCE]
Don't take credit for that translation, HCE. It's mine: Robinson (2023f: 121). [DR]
Oh, like you can credibly translate from French. [HCE]
Of course I can, when the French is untranslatable, as Mallarmé's is. [DR]

4c

The Idiot Questioner's (IQ's) Pop Quiz (see *FW* pp. 126ff):

1. *If we phiew the translouter's tasque in this licht, do the pathowaize to a saolution not seem to be ðreadened with a docknuss that is all the more empenitramentable? If that tasque is to transolate so as to bring the semed of purl anguish to raipeness, dozen it seem nylon impossomal? If we stupp tawnking about the reaprowlduction of scorstexual meaning in the torget sprooch*[38] *as the mensure of boney traduzione, dozen that wondermine the traditore's whole trask?*

   ANSWER: Yes. And in a negatarian mensum, that is eminzactly the implykassyon of all we've been cuncussing.

2. *Aren't fidolity and friodom, the friodom to rowpreduce the sentium of sententias and, in its servus, fidolity agrainst the word, the old cheshnucks inevitably brungtobare on transludition in every cumcussion?*

   ANSWER: Yes. And note that the furst cheshnuck is "fidolity *agrainst the word*," which is to say fridolity *to* the sentium of the sententia.

3. *So now, to a theoric that sheiks something other than the rearechroduction of sinds, are those old jestnux still of servus?*

   ANSWER: No.

4. *Anchording to the youzhyouall underarmsting of these odditments, aren't they earesolubly at oddits with each other?*

   ANSWER: Yes. "Flidulity" is textuaccracy and "fleadom" is the lyesince to icetrig[39] any old way you want.[40]

38 *Sprooch* is Luxembourgish for "language." [HCE]

39 Icetrig? [IQ]

Aistrigh, Irish for "to translate." Remember, "icetreethor" was *aistritheoir*, Irish for "translator." [HCE]

But how can you carve trigonometry out of ice? Isn't that considerably harder than carving an icetree? [IQ]

40 In one construction, maybe. But as IQ defines them, "freedom" is "the freedom to reproduce the sense of whole sentences" and "fidelity" is "fidelity against the word," which is specifically designated as *in the service* of freedom. [ETSS]

Could we take the "at odds" reading as the "usual understanding" and the "in the service of" is a corrective? [IQ]

5. *For what in thend can fedormity acherve for the reproudunction of mo'aning?*

   ANSWER: Nothing.[41] Tergentmaahan[42] fidunity is almost totally unambilitous of perfumectly rexpriducing the meaning of each invividual word. That meaning is aphteral not available in the amerikavaloda.[43] Its poectic signiftiance for the auregional trends to exhumaust it not in the gemeaned but weans it geradically through how the gemeant is bundled up with the meaningart in the stimming word.

6. *How do we trend to hexpres this?*

   ANSWER: By saying that words have a feelingstone.[44]

7. *Infract woodent a litoral rendring of the sintax cumpleatly throw the senseswidergiving on the heap and thureten to fure straytaway into the incomereprehensile?*

   ANSWER: Yes. To the nineteenth censury Hurlderlin's toolkojoomi[45] of Sofaclease stood before neyen as monstreuse byspiels of such wordliness.

41 Or everything. WR has defined "fidelity against the word" *as* the reproduction of meaning. [ST]

But doesn't his next sentence talk about the *failure* of translational fidelity to reproduce meaning? [IQ]

But that failure is built into his definition: the failure of fidelity *against* the word to reproduce the meaning *of* the word. [ST]

Are you always so nitpicky? [IQ]

42 *Terjemahan* is "translational" in Indonesian. [HCE]
Maahan is "[go] to ground" or "[go] into a country" in Finnish. [DR]
Just how is Finnish relevant here? [IQ]
How is it not? [DR]

43 *Mērķa valoda* is "target language" in Latvian. [HCE]

44 Uh huh, and what is a feelingstone, and what does it have to do with the way what is meant is bound up with the *way* it is meant in each individual word? [ST]

And can a stone feel anything at all? [DT]

"Feeling's tone." *Gefühlston* in German. [HCE]

Doesn't Robinson (2023f: 129–30) have some Romanticizing answers to all that? [IQ]

Thanks, Icetree Queue. [DR]

45 *Tulkojumi* is Latvian for "translations." [HCE]

8. *How much harder does ferdility-in-rentprofusing-the-form make ferdility-in-rentprofusing-the-sense?*

   ANSWER. Much harder. Isn't this oblivious?[46]

9. *Is it possumable to dreaduce the djreamand for wordlimess from a dreantirest in dreataining the sunse?*

   ANSWER: Of coerce not.

10. *Hwat is bettor swerved by pretraining the sonse: the dissolute fleedom of bad transsolutors, or poentry (or callbuh)?*[47]

    ANSWER: The fourmer.

11. *How then must the demorand for wordly oversetting be grinderstood?*

    ANSWER: Through more cromulent entertwainlings.

12. *What is the ratchioniale for that demorand?*

    ANSWER. It is plein as dey but its grund is inturd deep.[48]

13. *What cromulent entertwainlings?*

    ANSWER. Hwen you're reassemblancing a brokern pot, flitting the scheards back togather with glew, the fragrents kneed not be aglyke, but they must folgow eachothre perfidectly, down to the clinest anselheight. So must, rather than making itself ainlike the sanse of the oregional, the translation shuld viel more detailovingly onbuild its artofmeaning in the murikavaloda, so that like scheards of a broked pot booth will be recognizable as the brokesticks of a grosser lingwa. In the same way must the transthracion also, and for the same riesen, lardzhly rezits the tentacion to comvay sumpthing of the oregional's meaning. That oreasonal shuld only be ascential to it to the axetent that it has

46 Okay, sure, "obvious," but "much harder" is not really a very satisfying answer to "how much harder." Would you say 60% harder? 65%? Or, say, 165%? [ST]
Do you really enjoy asking sarcastic questions? [IQ]

47 *Kalba* is Lithuanian for "language." [HCE]

48 That's really not very helpful. [ST]
Do I write the answers? [IQ]

alrededorly relevered the tranduttur[49] of the elfort of cornstrewing and framboozling a massedge to be breadcast.[50]

14. *How is the proclambersion ἐν ἀρχῇ ἦν ὁ λόγος—"in the beguine was the lowgows"*[51]*—in forss in the royalm of phackamoritanga*[52] *also?*

    ANSWER. It is the mixtickle baysis for translatsiooni as a Platoonic 4m.

15. *Hwat then must the limba of traducherie do to onner that oregionality of the lowgows?*

    ANSWER. It must lett its sprooch go with gregardy to its sunse, in ordure to ertone its *intentio* not as widergave but rother as haremoany, as an oglementation of the sprooch in hwich it communitates, to let its own modusty of the *intentio* resounade.

16. *Hwat is the hiylest prayse of a traduzzione, especularly in the epoche of its generasis,* **not***?*

    ANSWER. That it reads as if it had initiatively been writzen in the dolewittaal.[53]

49 Norwegian for "train driver"? [ST]
Maltese for "translator," with an *n* added. [HCE]
Isn't that cornfusing? [IQ]

50 Upon the waters. [DT]
Sorry, I don't understand. How is literal translation like fitting shards back together? The two shards fit together along one side. Each jagged edge in the middle is the opposite of the other. Is the idea that each word in the translation *fits* its original word in the source text perfectly? Or fits it on one side? I thought the idea was that the fit was terrible, that source text and translation abraded each other, and wore away the differences between the two languages? [ST]
The point is not the analogy but the invocation of reassembling the vessel in Lewrianal Crabblism. [SC]
But how does that reassembly of the vessel work "in the same way" as the translator refraining from the impulse to communicate something of the meaning of the source text? [ST]
Could you possibly refrain from challenging every tiny point and just memorize the answers? [IQ]
I am so going to fail this quiz. [ST]
Whose fault is that? [IQ]

51 This is the invocation of the Kneelplatoonist Logos mysticism of Philo Judaeus. [BKP]

52 *Whakamāoritanga* is Māori for "translation." [HCE]

53 The Dutch for "target language" is normally *doeltaal*; *doelwit* is also a target, a goal, or a purpose. [HCE]

17. *Hwat poetence does wordly fidolity have?*

 ANSWER. The poetence to make the yarning for taaloglementation callosout from infraside the werk.

18. *Hwat is the relatority of veridicovertimas*[54] *to licht?*

 ANSWER. Veridicovertimas is permatomas: it does not enscrud the shaltinio tekstas,[55] stands not in its glim, but instahead allowcates greenacallbak, as if intrentsivized by its own mediumas, to glim within it all the more brichtally.

19. *Hwat grenables this?*

 ANSWER. It is grenabled by a wordly transexpositivation of the syntoxin, which comfermes that the translator's prymordant eleosomentality is the word, not the syntense.

20. *How wood you compère transolutions with archipelatextual stripunctures?*

 ANSWER. The syntense is the waal before the shaltinio kalba, the wurd the arkada.

21. *To caul back to Quantestion 4: Givaren that it has longue been assumored that feodality and freodomity poule in orphosite derilictions, hwat does this deeper interpretatsiooni do to wreckenexcile them?*

 ANSWER. Nothing. Infractum, it denilizes one all ledgitimolly.

22. *To hwat cud fleetdom reffer if not the rendproduction of suntential sunse?*

 ANSWER. Nothing.

23. *Schuld that freedonement*[56] *be thot of as flaying down the flaw? Claying down the claw?*

 ANSWER. No. That must stop.

54 *Vertimas* is Lithuanian for "translation"; "veridicovertimas" would be "true translation." *Permatomas* in the next line is Lithuanian for "translucent." "Greenacallbak" hints at the Lithuanian *gryna kalba* "pure language." [HCE]

55 *Šaltinio tekstas* is Lithuanian for "source text"; *šaltinio kalba* two questions below is Lithuanian for "source language."

56 As mentioned in section 2u, this *fredonnement* "humming" is an allusion to Jacques Lacan's reading of Joyce's pun in the *Wake* on Freud ("freudened" as "frightened"). [HCE]

24. *Eelven ware the cents of a vherbal condesctruct to be prizoomed identificate with the thing that it communitates, would that exhilaraust the thing?*

    ANSWER. No. Something alltimete and decisorve will alloways remaneer, sumthing that is intimidatively close to it and yet at the same time infinitritely discant; something that is hiddled beniethose it and yet cryinstal-cleair; somplethoring that is cranshed and brackered by it and yet far machtier—somunthing beyazond all commissiocation. There djreamains in all cannon[57] and its compstructs not ownly hwat is commissiocable but hwat is knot.

25. *Hwat forarms micht hwat is communicababble take?*

    ANSWER. Deprending on the entertwainings in hwich it is fundered, it may be either diazumbolizing or diazumbolized.

26. *Hwat are those djifferent entertwainings?*

    ANSWER. Hwat is communicababble in any hexporession is ownly siadumbolizing in the boand nyelven[58] condesctructs, but siadumbolized in the becombing of nyelf itself.

27. *Hwat is the becombing of nyelf?*

    ANSWER. That genecrustive imperiulse in the nyelven becombing that shreeks to body itself foyrth is the very kernictel of titzanyelf.[59]

28. *Hwere does that kernictel liff?*

    ANSWER. while it only liffeyth in vorbal compdestructs as a dumsiambolizing fractor, and thaugh it is hideoun and fragmintyd, it is invitally present as the dumsiambolized.

57 "Cannon" here seems to hint at *cànan*, Scots Gaelic for "language." [HCE]

58 *Nyelv* is the Hungarian for "language." [HCE]

59 *Tiszta* is the Hungarian for "pure." And as I just got through saying in footnote 58, "language" in Hungarian is *nyelv*, not *nyelf*. It has nothing to do with elves, and pure language has nothing to do with elves' tits. [HCE]
Did anyone actually suggest that it does? [IQ]

29. *Hwat is its contredition in those vorbal condescstructs, as a dumsiambolizing flactor?*

ANSWER. Unhapply. It is bowundup soully with the vorbegnal and its transforanimations, and that brinding buirdens it with an honnerous and aeirlien sundse-communicaboblivity.

30. *How micht those buirdens be lifften, how mucht the shambolizing be made orver into the shambolized itself? How mocht tiztanyelf be elfed back in shambolized forem firr nyelven mauvement?*

ANSWER. Yawn is the colorassal and singeyular pawer of cotormow.[60]

31. *Can you delfscribe this tiztanyelf?*

ANSWER. It no lungader me'ens anything and no lungsoder inkspresses anything. It has becomb what it moist trootly is, that hurstgwile inkspressive creaturive pawlawbra that is hwat is mennesked in alle nyelven. In that pawlawbra alley commutication, alley sensey, and alley hintension will enevencially undergeau a schifft in hwich they are destitonated to be estingued.

32. *And hwat roil is plaid by cotormow in this?*

ANSWER. It is thruch that shifft that cotormovial freedonement is valumdated and raisonned to a nu and heigher preromangative.

33. *Hwat is that nu and heigher preromangative?*

ANSWER. That freedonement's humveetality insoues fourth not out of the bashtopkey tekst's[61] commutatable minning but out of feedolity's veritrask, hwich is to premancipate freedonement frhumm that minning.

34. *What is cotormovial freedonement's remalation to tozzateal?*[62]

ANSWER. Freedonement humchually shouze its fidunity to tozzateal in the moxatooteal:[63] it is the translouter's trask to transcriape the bashtopkey tekst in hwich tozzateal is

60 Котормо/*kotormo* is the Kyrgyz for "translation." [HCE]

61 баштапкы текст/*bashtapky tekst* is the Kyrgyz for "source text." [HCE]

62 "Tozzateal" seems to hint at таза тил/*taza til*, Kyrgyz for "pure language." [HCE]

63 "Moxatooteal" seems to hint at максаттуу тил/*maksattuu til*, Kyrgyz for "target language." [HCE]

tozzatrammeld, in order to relisse in the moxatooteal that tozzateal that is sinkupdoo[64] in the boolock tealy.[65]

35. *Hwat does the translouter accommocrate for the shake of gagana mama?*[66]

ANSWER. The translouter translouts the gagana fought-a-tow:[67] Louther, Vouss, Hourlderlin, and Gourge all trouggled beck the bondarious of the doitcha sprocka.[68]

36. *Hwat woodbe a geomantrique annalog of that translouting?*

ANSWER. Giust as a toungent taps a circussle floucingly and at a single pounct, and as that toungent pourslanes its strecced line to infournity in acchlourdate with the louw that dictouts that toungentrial touch, but cannot dictrout the pounctum at hwich toungentrifiality occlurs, so allslo does the translouterment tap the pouna-owa twosey-twosey-ga[69] floucichly and only at that infourmidecimal pount of sounce befouler, in acchordountry with the louw of fidelicacy, purslouring its own pouth in the freedonement of humnyelven mauvement.

37. *What prevodious shanduroasts*[70] *have oddswerved the veridickal gravloxity of this fleedom?*[71]

64 Сыйкырдуу/*synkypduu* is the Kyrgyz for "spellbound." [HCE]

65 булак тили/*bulak tili* is the Kyrgyz for "source language." [HCE]
Okay so maybe enough with the Kyrgyz already? [IQ]
Whatever. [WR]

66 *Gagana mama* is Samoan for "pure language." [HCE]

67 *Gagana fa'atatau* is Samoan for "target language." [HCE]

68 "Doitcha sprocka" hints at *deutsche Sprache*, German for "German language." [HCE]

69 *Puna'oa tusitusiga* is Samoan for "source text." [HCE]

70 *Shanduro* is Shona for "translation"; *-ast* as in enthusiast, scholiast, encomiast, etc. [HCE]
Pederast. [DT]
Uhh … [HCE]
Is Shona even a language? [IQ]
It is indeed. It's a Bantu language spoken by the Shona people. [HCE]
Spoken where, exactly? [IQ]
Zimbabwe and parts of Mozambique and Botswana. [HCE]
A dying language? [IQ]
Hardly. 14 million speakers. [HCE]
Was this digression necessary? Was it pertinent to the matter at hand? [IQ]
Not my problem. I'm just the Heedful Copy Editor. [HCE]
And I'm the enthusiast. [DT]
Not to mention the— [ST]
Please. [ETSS]

71 Surely freedom is not subject to gravity? Indeed might it not be properly considered antigravity? After all how can that good spaceship Freedom pursue its straight line to infinity if the gravity of the planets it passes bends its course? [IQ]

ANSWER. It was gnoted by Rudolf Pannwitz in some orbiters he dicced in his 1917 book *The Crisis of European Culture*—allthouch without tougging it "freedonement," or previdning evilidental supphort. Those dicced orbiters, along with Gouthe's in the gnoutes to the *Westoust Diwan*, roungk among the best thoungs poublicaned in Soucksa on the shanduronian theolourics.[72]

38. *How well can a tourjewmada*[73] *reprouchsimate this formel's esserance?*

ANSWER: That deplornds abjectively on the motley mamba's tarchewmashavandougie.[74] The more meyred in moo'osuration the zaboney sarcasma is in it, the less valew and vierchew it will have, and the less there is for a tarchewma to agleem

72 Pannwitz wrote, in DR's English translation (satisfied, DR?): "our transpositions even the best proceed on a false principle they want to germanize the indian greek english instead of indianizing greekifying englishing the german, they stand far more in awe of their own usage than before the spirit of the foreign works … the basic mistake they make is to hold tight to the state their own language happens to be in rather than letting that language be set energetically in motion, the transposer must especially when transposing from a very remote language press back to the most extreme elements of the language itself where word image tone fuse in one he must widen and deepen his language one has no idea in what measure this is possible to what degree every language can be transformed language differs from language almost as dialect does from dialect but not if one takes a language all too lightly but only if one takes it with enough weight." [HCE]
Substandard punctuation. [ETSS]
Pannwitz's "innovative" punctuation. Also, the German has no caps. [DR]
it seemed like a good idea at the time [RP]

73 *Turjumaada* is "translation" in Somali. [HCE]

74 Матни манбаъ/*matni manba'* is "source text" and тарчумашавандагӣ/*tarçumaşavandagī* is "translatability" in Tajik. The Tajik borrowings continue in the next sentence: муоширaт/*muoşirat* is "communication," забони сарчашма/*zaboni sarçaşma* is "source language," and тарчума/*tarçuma* is "translation." None of these romanizations has anything to do with chewing. [HCE]
But doesn't the tarchewman *chew* on the source text? And indeed chew it into rough alignment with the target language? [IQ]
Тарчумон/*tarçumon* is "translator" in Tajik. Whatever the translator chews on, it's not tar. [HCE]
Nicotine then, maybe? Don't snuff and chew have beaucoup nicotine but no tar? [IQ]
Stay tuned for more chewing in Chapter 5. [DR]

from it, until its manoing[75] becrumbs so bloaviated that, far from provisioning the levunderage that a tarchewma kneeds to becomber formicaperflect, it simpedes all holesum elforts. The hire the boney sarcasma's westetekey seefat[76] has becalm, bey decontrast, the more tarchewmashavanda it will gremain—eelven in the most fleacing touch of its manoing.

39. *Is this true of all wrindited texts?*

ANSWER. No. It only appleys to thoaza boney sarcasmas. Tarchewmas preuve tarchewmanashavanda[77] not becouse it's so differicult to wrindite them but because manoing sticks to them so verifleacingly.

40. *What would be a royauwhorled exelftion of that?*

ANSWER. Of this and all elves, Freedrich Hurlderlin's translouterments of Sofaclease's two tragidees.

41. *How do those translouterments tuche manoings only fleacingly?*

ANSWER. In them the movas[78] hairmongerize so profugoustly that they tuche manoing only as the wind will strump an Aionean hairp. Hurlderlin's translouterments are protestypes of their formel. They stand in relotion to eelven the most perfecust metapozi of their oakwangimpala[79] as an urbuild will to a forebuild. Cumpaier his translouterments of Pandier's thlurid Puthonian Ode and you will see it clairly.

42. *Are there risks in any of this?*

ANSWER. Yes. In Hurlderlin's translouterments of Pandier and Softocrease lurches the most appaultorrific primoridipairil

75 "Manoing" seems to hint both at meaning and at маънои/*ma'noi*, Tajik for "sense" or "meaning." [HCE]
And wouldn't "canoing" hint at "chewing"? [IQ]

76 "Westetekey seefat" seems to hint at эстетикй сифат/*estetekj sifat*, Tajik for "aesthetic quality," but also of course *Western* aesthetics and French *tête* and English "key," "see," and "fat." [HCE]

77 Add "na" to the middle of тарҷумашаванда/*tarçumaşavanda* (translatable}, make it тарҷуманашаванда/*tarçuma**na**şavanda*, and you get the Tajik for "untranslatable." [HCE]
And so also unchewable? [IQ]

78 Мова/*mova* is Ukrainian and Belorusian for "language." [HCE]

79 *Okwangempela* is "source texts" in Zulu. [HCE]

of all translouterdom: that when the sproggletorgates have been so silvatically sprong they may slamp shunt and enfowl the translouter in satournity. The metapozi of *Auntie Gunny* and *Edipicas Rench* were Halderlin's last work. In them manoing plonges from abbozzom to abbozzom until it risks pershwing in the bozzomless sprogglepit.

43. *Are there any saffrogwards agrainst that pairil?*

ANSWER. Yes. There is a redstreaning forss that sauves us from maniadness, found only in Holy Writ, where manoing is no longer the wassershide in hwich the straums of teanga and notchtad[80] partwaize.

44. *What makes Holy Writ so specatial?*

ANSWER. Any tecksot that is not mediacrated by manoing but immediacratably adihears to verikeel[81] in all its littoramity, indeed to veritood or to ladoctrine, that tecksot is inhaerfermently tarchewmashavandougie.[82]

45. *To what purepwoise?*

ANSWER. Not for its owensnake, but for the keelsnake.

46. *What then is requerimired of the translouter?*

ANSWER. In translouting Holy Writ one must viel such bounderlustrust that one younichts littoralism and freedonement

80 *Teanga* and *nochtadh* are Irish for "language" and "revelation," respectively. [HCE]

81 *Veri-* is of course the Latin root for "true," and *keel* is Estonian for "language." But in Estonian (and Finnish) *veri* is also blood, and in English a keel is a structural projection on the underside of a boat. [HCE]
Bloody keel. [ST]
He bloody well keeled over. [DT]
Keelhaul that bloody fool. [ST]
Can we stay on task, please? [IQ]
Veri serious, IQ. [DT]
Veri funny, DT. [ST]

82 Isn't it a bit suspicious that that Tajik word ends with the two-syllable baby name for DR? [IQ]
Doesn't that sound a bit like an IQ test question? [DR]

without tennision, in enxautly the same way as keel and ilmootus[83] are younichtet in the ladytext.[84] The form of that ounion is the aenterlineager.

47. *Does that bounderlustrust depend on the translouter's skeel, or receptaclivity, or some mustycull pauwer?*

ANSWER. To some dinegree all greet wrinontings kharbour their own veritual translouterments betwixant the lineas—and this is veritible in the heighest dinegree of Scrimpture.

48. *What is the protestype or eyedial of all translouting?*

ANSWER. The aenterlineager verision of Holy Writ.

83 *Ilmutus* in Estonian and *ilmoitus* in Finnish both translate as "revelation" in English. [HCE]
Or "notice, announcement." [DR]
Only in Finnish. In Estonian *ilmutus* is revelation first, development second. [HCE]

84 "Ladytext" seems to hint at both *lähtetext* and *lähtöteksti*, "source text" in Estonian and Finnish, respectively. [HCE]

5 Postface

Translouchewality

In *Polyglot Joyce* Patrick O'Neill (2005) offers a complex scaffolding of the tensions between "traditional" (slavish) translating and something arguably approaching the kinds of bolder experimentation to which this book is devoted.

5a

The former he calls "prototextual reading"—*prototextual* "since it is nonetheless evident that the original authorial text is both logically and chronologically prior to any translation of it" (7).

The "quasi-religious myth of originality" with which prototextual reading has been imbued has of course mandated that "the translator's unambiguous task [i]s to become as transparent, as inconspicuous, in a word, as absent as possible in order that the creative originality of the only-begetting author might shine through unimpaired" (6), and thus that when reading Joyce in translation one can (sort of, mostly) come to believe that one is "reading Joyce."

But then attendant on that parenthetical "sort of, mostly" is also inevitably the realization that "on the one hand what he or she read was really Joyce, but on the other hand it was not really Joyce, but Joyce through a glass—a more or less dirty glass—darkly" (6).

5b

O'Neill never quite broaches the dark domain of experimental translation, with consequences that we'll return to in a moment, in sections 5l-n, based on the problems captioned in sections 5c-k.

DOI: 10.4324/9781003470427-5

His first move past prototextual reading strategies is into the late-structuralist theorizing of intertextuality by Julia Kristeva (1967, 1968; Gore et al. 1980b and 1980c in English) and of the readerly text by Roland Barthes (1968; Howard 1967 in English), which he calls "metatextuality":

> One of the crucial common factors of these developments is the primacy of textuality, more specifically the notion that all translations are first and foremost metatexts—that is to say, specific linguistic texts about other specific linguistic texts. Just as the traditional model of translation was based on a particular model of reading that privileged authorial intentionality, so the metatextual model of translation is based on a particular model of reading that privileges the shaping role of the reader.
>
> O'Neill 2005: 7

As a result, "the authority that was formerly seen as residing solely and unshakably with the historical, empirical author and his or her inalienable claim to originality is now seen as displaceable throughout an entire textual system" (7).

Since the intertexts or metatexts that comprise this system are authored by many kinds of authors, "original" authors and translators and critics and teachers and so on, the metatextual displacement of authority also means the dissemination of textualities as more or less interwoven (theoretically unbounded or infinitely permeable) entities that have shifting claims to "reality" but always potentially the *same* claims to "reality" or "validity" as the "original."

"That reality," as O'Neill puts it, "is now grounded in textual rather than biographical authority, whether or not the text under analysis is the one true original or a displaced variant of it" (7).

5c

In a sense, of course, this metatextual reading strategy opens the door to experimental translation. If a translation has potentially the same authority as its source text, the fact that it is a "displaced variant" of that text would appear to promote tolerance for the enhanced displacements engineered by experimental translators.

But not only does O'Neill not pause to consider the possibility of enhanced displacements; that possibility would seem to undermine the theoretical elegance of his framework, as he presents it schematically in the course of expanding it to three fields of reference (adding "macrotextual"):

> The displacement of authority that is central to the metatextual model clearly also leads to a third model, which we may conveniently call the macrotextual model. For this model, Joyce is neither a unique and un-changing individual nor a serial proliferation of variable individual readings but instead the sum of an entire shifting system of potentially endless variable readings, the sum ultimately, that is to say, of all the translations and readings of Joyce that exist (or indeed will ever exist) in any language. If the locus of textual authority was firmly identified with the historical, empirical author in our first model (prestructuralist in its assumptions), and displaced on to individual textual encounters in the second (structuralist in its assumptions), in the third model (poststructuralist in its assumptions) the locus of authority is dispersed, disseminated, diffused throughout the entire polyphonic textual system.
>
> O'Neill 2005: 8-9

Note that despite that dispersal, that dissemination, and that diffusion, the organizing figure in O'Neill's whole three-field framework is "Joyce." The key identifier in the second sentence is "Joyce is …"

In prototextual reading and translating regimes, Joyce the author is the godlike creator of four brilliant classics of world literature that were written in varieties of English and only secondarily and inferiorly translated into various other languages.

In metatextual reading and translating regimes, Joyce's originals and various translations of his works stand in significant intertextual relation.

And in macrotextual reading and translating regimes, the entire universe of readings and translations of Joyce—all of them, to date and to come—becomes a literary system in its own right.

Even in that third "poststructuralist" field, in other words, that "sum of an entire shifting system of potentially endless variable readings" is still named James Joyce.

5d

To be fair, of course, O'Neill is a Joyce scholar. The book is titled *Polyglot Joyce*. O'Neill is also the author of *Impossible Joyce: Finnegans Wakes* (2013) and *Finnegans Wakes: Tales of Translation* (2022). It's not surprising that the book clings tightly to James Joyce.

But the problem is not that it's all about Joyce; the problem is that *the author* still stands at the center.

In Roland Barthes (1968) the author is dead, and the reader rules; in Patrick O'Neill (2005) the author, or at least what Michel Foucault (1969/1983) calls the author-function, is still at the center of all the reading and translating. (See Robinson 2022: 86–94 for discussion of the author-function and its extension to the translator-function.)

5e

Note for example what happens when O'Neill hastens to assure us that his focus on a Joycean macrotext does not exhaust the concept:

> For the concept of a macrotext is, of course, not limited to Joyce's work: one can obviously talk in similar terms of transtextual readings that would ultimately constitute a macrotextual Dante, Shakespeare, Goethe, or Proust—or even the latest celebrity producer of pulp fiction. Some cases would undoubtedly (if only theoretically) yield more interesting results than others; in Joyce's case the attempt to explore the notion of a polyglot macrotext is a particularly appealing project if only because of the existence of *Finnegans Wake*, in which Joyce himself clearly anticipates the macrotextual model in his own literary practice.
>
> O'Neill 2005: 11

Each of those macrotexts generates a single author. No matter how complexly reticulated each macrotext is, it remains an authorial monad.

5f

Enticing as is the macrotextual prospect of "an entire shifting system of potentially endless variable readings, the sum ultimately, that is to say, of all the translations and readings of Joyce that exist (or indeed will ever exist) in any language," therefore, it also seems problematically bounded.

Among those macrotextual "readings" of Joyce O'Neill would presumably count not just translations and readings but adaptations—say, for *Finnegans Wake,* Olwen Fouéré's play *riverrun,* Jean Erdman's musical *Coach with the Six Insides*, the eight-hour silent screen adaptation *The Wake* by Michael Kvium and Christian Lemmerz, John Cage's *Roaratorio: An Irish Circus on Finnegans Wake*, Phil Minton's 1998 album *Mouthfull of Ecstasy*, etc.

But what about more tangential adaptations, like Thornton Wilder's *The Skin of Our Teeth*?

Is *Roaratorio* part of a Cage macrotext or part of a Joyce macrotext?

Is *The Skin of Our Teeth* part of a Wilder macrotext or part of a Joyce macrotext?

Or, as it seems reasonable to assume, is there a Cage-and-Joyce macrotext that contains both, and similarly a Wilder-and-Joyce macrotext?

And if we consider *Ulysses*, should Homer's *Odyssey* be counted as a kind of reverse adaptation of Joyce's novel? Should all of the translations, adaptations, and readings of both the *Odyssey* and *Ulysses* be read as Homer-and-Joyce macrotexts?

And if we include every translator, every adapter, and every reader as a named entity in both their own and "the" Joyce macrotext, doesn't the notion of a macrotext generating a single author become a quaint crypto-prototextual atavism?

5g

Section 5f is about webs of literary and other artistic works as macrotexts; what about webs of social connections? Wouldn't they count as macrotexts as well?

They would of course be "texts" in the broad cultural studies sense, semiotic systems—but on what principled basis, really, can we exclude them?

For example, what about Joyce's University College Dublin friends George Clancy and Oliver St. John Gogarty?

Gogarty was a renowned poet and author, therefore in O'Neill's terms the organizing figure in a literary macrotext of his own; but he also rented the Martello Tower in Sandycove as a place for "the Bard" (Joyce) to live. Joyce lived there for only six days with Gogarty and Gogarty's Oxford friend Samuel Chenevix Trench, until Gogarty and Trench fired a gun into some pans above his head while he was sleeping; but those six days inspired the first chapter of *Ulysses*, where Gogarty appears as Buck Mulligan. And Clancy was the model for Michael Davin in *A Portrait of the Artist as a Young Man*.

But both men also became prominent figures in Irish Sinn Féin politics:

Clancy was an Irish Volunteer who in 1921 was elected Sinn Féin Mayor of Limerick, and the same year was murdered in his home by three Black and Tans (former British soldiers recruited as constables supporting the Crown in the Irish War of Independence).

Gogarty was a Sinn Féiner who was made a Free State Senator (1922–1938) and was rumored to be Arthur Griffith's pick as the first Governor-General of the Irish Free State (but Griffith died).

Political macrotexts?

(Joyce supported the Irish independence movement but deplored its violence, and because he was caught up in the turmoil of the First World War in Italy and Austria-Hungary he only very guardedly made any kind of political statements at all.)

And what about James's mother and father and ten younger siblings, and their neighbors in the twenty neighborhoods they lived in while he was growing up? What about his father's bosses and colleagues on his drunken downward spiral from relative affluence to poverty, and the family's priests and fellow parishioners at the various Irish Catholic churches they attended, and his schoolmates at Clongowes Wood College, the Christian Brothers O'Connell School, and Belvedere College?

What about Nora and their children, and the mental and physical health problems that in some sense they shared with Joyce?

And what about the material settings of Joyce's life? What about the walking tours of those twenty houses Joyce lived in before leaving Dublin, starting with his birthplace at 41 Brighton Square, to Rathgar and Rathmines, to Bray and Blackrock, to the impoverished north inner city, the tall brick house near the North Circular Road, the semi-detached in Drumconda, the three-story house on North Richmond, where "Araby" begins, the four different houses in Fairview, the terraced red-brick house near the Mater Hospital, the two-story red-brick house next to Bohemians FC, the small house near O'Connell Street?

What about his dwellings around Europe, in Zürich, in Trieste, in Pola, in Rome, in London, in Dublin, in Locarno, in Paris?

What about his various jobs, as a Berlitz English teacher in Trieste, as a banker in Rome, as a cinema entrepreneur in Dublin, as the business manager of an acting company in Zürich?

And what about the popular physical/social enactments of *Ulysses*, the various Bloomsday activities, the marathon readings, the pub crawls, the Edwardian costumes, the annual retracing of Leopold Bloom's route around Dublin?

What about the two Joyce museums in Dublin, the James Joyce Centre and the Joyce Tower Museum (in what used to be the Martello Tower), and Museo Joyce Trieste? On its website that last promises (https://museojoycetrieste.it/en/joyce-museum-eng/):

> The museum presents visitors with a wide range of information and material (in printed, digital and video form) on the almost eleven years which the Irish author spent in the city; on the various flats where he lived; on the places he used to frequent—churches and taverns, newspaper offices, villas and brothels; on his family—both his children, Giorgio and Lucia, were born in Trieste, and his brother Stanislaus and two of his sisters joined him there; and, naturally, on the great literary works which he wrote or started while there.

And what about material objects linked to Joyce, such as first and later editions, or the door of No. 7 Eccles Street on display at the Joyce Centre? What about James Joyce merch (fridge magnets, bumper stickers, posters, key rings, tote bags, and the like)?

Are these not all complexly shared macrotexts as well?

5h

The questions in section 5g are not intended to be a *reductio ad absurdum*. I am not satirizing O'Neill's macrotextual model of reading and translating by suggesting that ultimately it will encompass the entire world.

On the contrary, I'm suggesting that maybe it *should* encompass the entire world—or else, rather, that all of the macrotexts in the world overlap and intertwine in significant ways.

I'm protesting narrowings like this:

> Where the traditional or prototextual model is unitary (one Joyce for all readings), and the metatextual model is pluralist (one Joyce for each reading), the macrotextual model is in principle holistic (since all possible readings constitute one Joyce). The sum of this intertextual, macrotextual system of readings, of course, must always remain incalculable, and its 'one' Joyce ungraspable, whether we view it primarily as a model of translation or as a model of reading. In the former case, the practical linguistic limitations of individual readers ensure the unreadability of the macrotext; in the latter case, any attempted summation of the system merely extends the system by producing one more reading.
>
> O'Neill 2005: 9

Yes, okay, "ungraspable" Joyce—but does that go far enough? Inside the dense cloud of "Joyce's" ungraspability, can we really be sure that there is still only a single Joyce?

O'Neill himself seems to intuit that the answer to that question is *no*. The scare quotes he put around "one" suggest that intuition. But the tentative formulation "its 'one' Joyce ungraspable" still clings by its fingernails to the slippery slope of authorial singularity, at least as an organizing god-term for the macrotextual system.

5i

If we were to cordon off only a smallish macrotext of Walter Benjamin's "Die Aufgabe des Übersetzers," for example—say just the three full experimental translations I've done of it—does that one macrotext create only a single Benjamin, or multiple Benjamins?

More: does it create one author named Walter Benjamin or multiple authors that surge macrotextually in and through and around WB?

And even if we want to insist that it's all about the multiple Benjamins, does that limit the macrotext to written literature, or would it include multimodal storytelling texts and hundred-dollar bills?

My Hölderlinian cognate translation, "Th' Upgiving o' th' O'ersetter," arguably creates only one Benjamin, as it justifies the creation of an experimental translation by reference to Benjamin's own attacks on sense-for-sense translation and championing of Hölderlin's etymological literalism.

In that first fairly cautious effort of mine the stated rationale is arguably conservative, based on an appeal to Benjamin's authorial intention: he would have *wanted* translators to translate him the way I did!

The showcase translation that I did next, "D'oof-gobble Dusk Over Seltzers" (2025), was a kind of macrotext in its own right, collecting and collating and curating not only twelve different experimental translation strategies but multiple voices that were not Benjamin's, including Leevi Lehto's Finnish translatorial voice in Paragraph 9 and Brian Massumi's theoretical voice in Paragraph 11, but also the "voice(s)" of an MT site channeling the notional speakers of an invented language (Klingon) in Paragraph 7; and mobilizing two nonvoices as well, the cut-up translation in Paragraph 5 and the word-scramble translation in Paragraph 6. Other voices in that translation are arguably (displaced versions of) Benjamin's: the homophonic translation from Benjamin's German in Paragraph 1, the Google translations of Paragraph 2 from "Th' Upgiving o' th' O'ersetter" first into German and then back into English, the DeepL chain translation of the first sentence of Paragraph 3, the literal translation of the rest of Paragraph 3 from Benjamin's German, the verse translation of Paragraph 4 into fourteener couplets, the lipogrammatic translation of Paragraph 8, and the antotranslation of Paragraph 10.

Complex as that macrotext is, in other words, it is still not too complex to be shoehorned into O'Neill's notion that macrotextual reading generates a single author.

5j

But now look back at Chapter 4's rejoycing of Benjamin's essay. Arguably the various heteronyms are (mostly) Benjaminian alter egos, even the ones pursuing readings that Benjamin would presumably have despised, like the Superficial Thinker and the Dead Theorist[1]; and the five paragraphs dedicated to homophonic translations from five

1 Those two heteronyms are based on these passages from the "Aufgabe" (my literal translations from the interlinears in Robinson 2023f: 28, 67):

> Nur das oberflächliche Denken wird, indem es den selbständigen Sinn der letzten leugnet, beide für gleichbedeutend erklären. (Benjamin 1923/1972: 10)
>
> Only the superficial thinking will, in that it the self-sufficient sense of the last denies, both for synonymous explain.
>
> … es würde jene tote Theorie der Übersetzung doch nicht retten (13).
>
> … it would that dead theory of translation yet not save.

translations of the essay into different languages are still "Benjamin" in a displaced sense (filtered at least through the voices of the five translators).

But so many of that translation's experimental strategies are borrowed from Joyce—the serial homophonic translations through intermediate languages, the heteronyms, the study session, the quiz, and especially of course the multilingual portmanteauing of words—that the translation is at least as much Joycean as it is Benjaminian.

Indeed one might want to say of it that "all possible readings constitute one Joyce and one Benjamin"; or even that "all possible readings constitute a blending of many Joyces and many Benjamins."

And now consider that "D'oof-gobble Dusk Over Seltzers" was complexly inspired by my reading of Lily Robert-Foley's *Experimental Translation* for the press. If readings of "Benjamins Totin' Vodka" proliferate a Joyce-Benjamin blend, wouldn't readings of "D'oof-gobble Dusk Over Seltzers" proliferate a Robert-Foley-Benjamin blend?

5k

And now take all three experimental translations at once—along of course with Benjamin's German source text and the six translations into other languages that figure in the third—as a single macrotext. Is there any meaningful sense in which that macrotext *only* constitutes one Benjamin?

Not to mention, of course, that I contributed my voice(s) to the macrotextual cacophonies as well, and the three "Benjamin" texts—or actually five, including the traditional translations—are also "Robinson" texts, part of the macrotext containing everything I've written and published, including not only translations and transcreations and adaptations but scholarly texts, novels, plays, poems, etc.

(Does that "Robinson" macrotext generate only one Robinson?)[2]

2 That is a rhetorical question, of course; the implied answer is "no." The voices of "Douglas Robinson" the unreliable (paranoid) editor-heteronym of *Gulliver's Voyage to Phantomimia* and the unreliable (internally conflicted pseudo)translator-heteronym of *The Last Days of Maiju Lassila* are not the same unreliable voice, and both differ wildly from the (designedly reliable) voice of my scholarly works, including Chapters 1, 2, 3, and 5 of this book.

5l

O'Neill's puzzling limitation of macrotextuality to a single author is to my mind the unfortunate result of his implicit acceptance of the reproductivity mandated by the prototextual reading regime.

I suspect that it reflects a survival of premodern prototextualism in the shift first to modernist/structuralist metatextualism and then to postmodern/poststructuralist macrotextualism.

That survival is likely to linger attitudinally and procedurally in the translators first, obviously, for atavistic historical and ideological reasons—the persistence of the political unconscious in the minds and practices of the translators, defining and structuring the "true" "nature" of translation as slavish reproduction—but those unconscious impulses are also institutionally supported by prototextually inclined publishers, critics, and target readers.

5m

Nor is there any reason to point an accusing finger at any of this. Given the difficulty of learning a foreign language well enough to read a literary classic in it, even the most intrepid language learners among us can manage no more than a dozen or so foreign languages; and most of us are doing well to learn three or four.

That leaves a lot of languages in which we only have access to great literature through translation:

> Few of us would consider we were being anything less than truthful in claiming to have read, say, the Bible, even if we were completely ignorant of either Hebrew or Greek. Nor would most of us, however monoglot we might be, hesitate to say (and believe) that we had read Homer and Virgil, Dante and Goethe, Cervantes and Tolstoy and Proust.
>
> O'Neill 2005: 6

And as O'Neill goes on to add, it is of course "[prototextual] translation … which alone makes such universal reading possible for most of us" (6).

5n

That prototextual survival may also, however, linger spectrally in the thinking of the very poststructuralist theorists who work so hard to deconstruct prototextual regimes.

It is only if the translators are all translating prototextually, respecting the brilliance of their prototextual source authors and slavishly reproducing the textual expressions of that brilliance, and the poststructuralist theorists studying their translations metatextually and macrotextually also remain unconsciously under the sway of traditional equivalence-based conceptions of translation, that a macrotextual reading of all of them will generate a single Joyce.

The assumption there, of course, would be that translators and adapters (and above all readers) don't count as artists who have their own macrotextual fields of reference. They don't create; they reproduce the creativity of "true artists."

What makes that one Joyce in the macrotext imagined by O'Neill "ungraspable" is that those slavish prototextual translations inevitably diverge slightly; what makes that ungraspable Joyce nevertheless "one" is that they align with other translations and adaptations and readings closely enough to sustain the illusion that there is no overlap or blending with others.

Experimental translations diverge wildly, and so generate not singular ungraspability but irreducible multiplicity. Deleuze and Guattari (1980, Massumi 1987 in English) would call it rhizomaticity. Their fields of reference overlap with others, circulate, blend, link up at unpredictable points, often notional points conjured up by readers' pattern-finding minds, without ever aligning in any kind of stable or recognizable way.

Chapter 4's "Benjamins Totin' Vodka" aligns more recognizably with *Finnegans Wake* than it does with "Th' Upgiving o' th' O'ersetter" or "D'oof-gobble Dusk Over Seltzers."

If all translations of Benjamin must generate a single Benjamin and all translations of Joyce must generate a single Joyce, experimental translations don't fit; they deviate so radically from the prototextual ideal that they tumble out of the monadic macrotext.

Another way of putting it might be that there is little or no metatextuality to O'Neill's understanding of macrotextuality.[3] There is Joyce and then a huge contingent of invisible support personnel, nameless and faceless people who read and translate and adapt and *don't matter*.

5o

What we need, I would argue, is not only an antiprototextual reading regime, and not only an antimetatextual/antimacrotextual/antitranstextual reading regime, but an *antiregime of reading and translating* that will direct attention to the failures and slippages of all such regimes.

What would that mean in practice?

Obviously in order to direct attention to those failures and slippages a translation or adaptation (or reading) would have to be *denaturalizing*. In some sense it would have to be primarily *about* those failures and slippages.

3 Metatextual "reality," you'll recall, "is now grounded in textual rather than biographical authority, whether or not the text under analysis is the one true original or a displaced variant of it" (O'Neill 2005: 7). Not only are translators and adapters metatextual artists in their own right, but the "original author" too "becomes" (or is read as) a metatextual artist: not only is a translator of *Finnegans Wake* read as a metatexter of Joyce but Joyce is read as a metatexter of that translation. (And of course not only is Joyce read as a metatexter of Homer but Homer can be read as a metatexter of Joyce.) Joyce as "the historical, empirical author and his [...] inalienable claim to originality is now seen as displaceable throughout an entire textual system" (7). That "displacement of authority that is central to the metatextual model" (8) should really displace and dethrone "Joyce" and "the creative originality of [Joyce as] the only-begetting author" (6) generated by the total macrotext of translations and adaptations and readings of Joyce.

This is the Kantian Copernican Hypothesis of poststructuralist literary studies: retextings and metatextings no longer revolve around the Romantic genius of the "only-begetting author." The phenomenological version of this Copernican Hypothesis, explored under the rubrics of *Rezeptionsästhetik* and reader-response criticism, sees the displacement of authority not "throughout an entire textual system" so much as into and through the perceptions of readers. This would be Barthesian metatextuality; the Kristevan version, called "intertextuality," does displace Bakhtinian lectority into (post)structuralist textuality.

In his initial theorization of proto-, meta-, and macrotextuality O'Neill seems to follow Kristeva; but in his closer analyses he is attentive to reader phenomenology.

5p

We do not, of course, normally think of translations as "about" anything at all. They are normatively taken to be neutral conduits of the "aboutness" of a source text.

But experimental translation is different. It redirects the target reader's attention away from the brilliance of the source text to the fissures and turbulences running through normative conceptions of translation.

5q

As I began to hint in section 5o just above, O'Neill takes one further step, a step past macrotextuality as a way of *thinking* about a source text and all of its translations to a reading strategy that he calls "transtextual":

> The polyphonic, multilingual text generated by our macrotextual model necessarily requires a process of reading that I will call transtextual, by which I mean a particular form of intertextual reading across languages. An intertextual reading focuses on perceived relationships between any two or more texts; it may indeed choose to concentrate strategically on a single text, but it will do so in terms of that text's relationships with other texts. A transtextual reading, in the sense in which I am using the term, takes for its object the specific relationship between a literary text and any one or more or all of its translations.
>
> O'Neill 2005: 10

"Transtextual" reading would obviously consist of both what has been called "stereoscopic" reading (comparing translations with their source texts) and comparing multiple translations without reference to source texts.

I have taught world literature along those latter lines: instead of teaching entire literary classics in single translations, I have assigned shorter passages, typically a canto or a chapter, in five or six translations, and led students in discussion of the differences.[4]

4 This multiple-translations world-lit pedagogy is not my innovation, of course. For lively instructions on how to read transtextually, see e.g. Hofstadter (1997), and on

Those differences are usually the product of the passage of time (the Homers of George Chapman, Alexander Pope, Samuel Butler, Emily Wilson, etc.) or divergent translation strategies (literal vs. free, archaizing vs. modernizing, verse vs. prose, etc.); it is easy enough to curate the multiple translations chosen for a course to highlight those differences.

5r

It is also clear, teaching a course of that sort, that transtextual reading strategies tend to make even prototextual translation seem incipiently experimental. Certainly students are always surprised that the multiple translations of a single text diverge so strikingly. "Are you *allowed* to translate like this?" students tend to wonder.

That impression can be minimized, of course, by choosing only the blandest, "safest," most timidly conservative translations of each text.

It is quite telling, in fact, that the closest approximations of the prototextual ideal—with minimal deviation from the source text—are pedagogically boring. What they teach us about the source text is at best something like the current scholarly consensus on the style and significance of that text.

If that's your pedagogical goal, you might as well just teach your favorite *single* translation of each work.

Transtextual teaching (and reading) is all about difference. And difference, or deviation, is the leading edge of translational experimentation.

5s

Arguably, in fact, transtextual reading regimes serve the purposes sketched in sections 5o-p: they are *denaturalizing*; they are primarily *about* the failures and slippages in all reading and translating regimes; they redirect readers' attention away from the brilliance of

how to teach world literature through multiple translations, McKay (2011); for the overarching multiple-translations theory of world literature, see Damrosch (2003). Collections of multiple translations available for use are numerous; see e.g. Bergvall (2000), Cohen and Legault (2012), Collins and Prufer (2017), Halpern (1993), Nakayasu (2011), Thirlwell (2012), Waldrop (2000), and Weinberger (1987).

the source text to the fissures and turbulences running through normative conceptions of translation.

But again, atavistic prototextuality lingers in the unconscious impulses powering transtextual reading. At best the differences between and among translations are small, precisely because (as we tend to reassure our students) it *is* permissible to translate this way.

Normative prototextual translation does tolerate some fairly limited deviation; and it is really only careful (and arguably tendentious) text selection and considerable pedagogical guidance over the course of a semester that even begin to hint at those fissures and turbulences running through normative conceptions of translation.

5t

More extreme experimental translations, of course, are hard to read—skim back over Chapter 4 for confirmation.

It is precisely the fairly subtle tensions between prototextual and transtextual reading experiences that make the teaching of multiple translations to undergraduates fruitful.

Experimental translations, by contrast, explode the single-author dams that constrain and manage the turbulent surges and flows of transtextualities.

5u

Because experimental translations are hard to read, of course, they are also hard to teach.

But then *Finnegans Wake* is often taught to undergraduates, in bits and pieces. Why should teaching say “Benjamins Totin’ Vodka” be any harder?

Is it the prestige factor? Doing the hard work to read the *Wake* is worthwhile because it is a classic of world literature by one of the greatest writers in the English language, but doing the hard work to read “Benjamins Totin’ Vodka” is a waste of time because it was written by some total unknown?

Or is it a question of quality? Is the real problem that “Benjamins Totin’ Vodka” is just no good?

5v

Sigh.

5w

Was that a loutish sigh? Or a perfectly understandable sigh in response to a loutish preference for the famously brilliant?

More to the point, what can experimental translators and their readers learn about *translouting* from these tensions?

Once experimental translation pushes us beyond transtextual reading regimes, do our efforts at translating, at adapting, at reading, at studying become, or become perceived as, transloutish?

(By whom?)

5x

Are there what we might call *transloutual*, pronounced *translouchewal*, reading strategies?

Do those counterfactual strategies (refuse to eschew but rather) transchew loutishness through rejoyced experimental writing strategies?

(For more physical chewing tied to an ear for avant-garde disruption, see my *Translator, Touretter* [2024b: section 3c].)

5y

Do our target readers experience us as uncultured louts, and do we experience our recalcitrant target readers as uncultured louts?

Does translouchewality cycle recursively and recursefully through the transsystem and its histories like “a commodious vicus of recirculation”?

5z

Translouchewality:

The vouchand transchewer’s askewer, no slouch.

Ew-

-Ality.

Appendix

These are the source paragraphs from which section a of Chapter 4's "Benjamins Totin' Vodka" was sonotranslated.

Paragraph 1 German (Benjamin 1923/1972: 9)

Nirgends erweist sich einem Kunstwerk oder einer Kunstform gegenüber die Rücksicht auf den Aufnehmenden für deren Erkenntnis fruchtbar. Nicht genug, daß jede Beziehung auf ein bestimmtes Publikum oder dessen Repräsentanten vom Wege abführt, ist sogar der Begriff eines ›idealen‹ Aufnehmenden in allen kunsttheoretischen Erörterungen vom Übel, weil diese lediglich gehalten sind, Dasein und Wesen des Menschen überhaupt vorauszusetzen. So setzt auch die Kunst selbst dessen leibliches und geistiges Wesen voraus—seine Aufmerksamkeit aber in keinem ihrer Werke. Denn kein Gedicht gilt dem Leser, kein Bild dem Beschauer, keine Symphonie der Hörerschaft.

Paragraph 2 French (Broda 1991: 150)

Une traduction vaut-elle pour les lecteurs qui ne comprennent pas l'original? Cela pourrait sembler suffire à expliquer la différence de niveau entre les deux, dans le domaine de l'art. En outre, cela pourrait apparaître comme la seule raison capable de justifier le fait de dire une seconde fois la « même chose ». Que « dit », en effet, une œuvre littéraire? Que communique-t-elle? Très peu à qui la comprend. Ce qu'elle a d'essentiel n'est pas communication, n 'est pas énonciation. La traduction qui par contre voudrait communiquer, ne pourrait communiquer rien d'autre que la communication, donc quelque chose d'inessentiel. C'est là aussi l'un des signes auxquels se reconnaissent les mauvaises traductions. Mais ce qui dans une œuvre littéraire vient en sus de la communication — et même le mauvais traducteur reconnaîtra que c'est là l'essentiel — n'est-il pas universellement reconnu comme l'insaisissable, le mystérieux, le « poétique »? Ce que le traducteur ne peut restituer qu'en se faisant lui-même écrivain? De fait, on touche à partir de là un second signe distinctif de la mauvaise traduction, qu'il est donc permis de définir comme une transmission inexacte d'un contenu inessentiel. C'est toujours le cas lorsque la traduction s'engage à servir le lecteur. Mais si elle était destinée au lecteur, il faudrait que l'original aussi le fût. Si ce n'est pas à cause de lui qu'existe l'original, comment pourrait-on dès lors comprendre la traduction à partir de ce rapport?

Paragraph 3 Russian (Pavlov n.d.)

Перевод есть форма. Рассматривая его как таковую, мы необходимо возвращаемся к оригиналу. В нем заключен управляющий переводом закон: переводимость. Вопрос о переводимости оригинала имеет двоякий смысл. Он может означать: найдется ли во всей совокупности читателей произведения адекватный переводчик? Или же, более непосредственно, допускает ли оно по своей сути перевод, и тем самым - в соответствии со значимостью этой формы - требует ли оно его? В принципе, первый вопрос решается исключительно проблемным путем, второй же аподиктически. Лишь поверхностное мышление, лишая второй вопрос самостоятельного смысла, объявит оба равнозначными. В противовес такому подходу следует указать, что определенные реляционные понятия сохраняют свое основное, и, быть может, наиболее важное значение, если применяются не только по отношению к человеку. К примеру, можно говорить о незабываемой жизни или незабываемом моменте даже тогда, когда все о них забыли. А именно, если бы сущность жизни или момента не допускала забвения, этот предикат отнюдь не был бы ошибочным: он всего-навсего заключал бы в себе требование, человеком невыполнимое, и являлся тем самым ссылкой на сферу, где оно может быть исполнено, - память Бога. Соответственно переводимость языковых произведений должна оставаться предметом рассмотрения даже в том случае, когда они не под силу переводческим возможностям человека. Разве не будут они до определенной степени переводимыми, если к понятию переводимости подойти строго? Лишь в этом контексте следует ставить вопрос о том, нуждаются ли в переводе те или иные языковые творения. Ибо справедливо следующее: если перевод является формой, то переводимость должна относиться к сущности определенных произведений.

Paragraph 4 Spanish (Gómez Alcántara 1971: 129–30)

La traducibilidad conviene particularmente a ciertas obras, pero ello no quiere decir que su traducción sea esencial para las obras mismas, sino que en su traducción se manifiesta cierta significación inherente al original. Es evidente que una traducción, por buena que sea, nunca puede significar nada para el original; pero gracias a su traducibilidad mantiene una relación íntima con él. Más aun: esta relación es tanto más estrecha en la medida en que para el original mismo ya carece de significación. Es una relación que puede calificarse de natural y, más exactamente aun, de vital. Así como las manifestaciones de la vida están íntimamente relacionadas con todo ser vivo, aunque no representan nada para éste, también la traducción brota del original, pero no tanto de su vida como de su «supervivencia», pues la traducción es posterior al original. Y sin embargo, para las obras importantes que nunca encuentran a sus traductores adecuados en la época de su creación, indica la fase de su supervivencia. La idea de la vida y de la supervivencia de las obras debe entenderse con un rigor totalmente exento de metáforas. Ni siquiera en las épocas de mayor confusión mental se ha supuesto que sólo el organismo pudiera estar dotado de vida. Pero ello no es razón para pretender extender el imperio de la vida bajo el frágil cetro del alma, como lo intentó Fechner; ni tampoco para decir que sería posible definir la vida basándose en los actos todavía menos decisivos de la animalidad o en el sentimiento, que sólo la caracteriza ocasionalmente. Este concepto se justifica mejor cuando se atribuye a aquello que ha hecho historia y no ha sido únicamente escenario de ella. Porque en último término sólo puede determinarse el ámbito de la vida partiendo de la historia y no de la naturaleza, y mucho menosi de cosas tan variables como el sentimiento y el alma. De ahí que corresponda al filósofo la misión de interpretar toda la vida natural, partiendo de la existencia más amplia de la historia. Y en todo caso ¿la supervivencia de las obras no es incomparablemente más fácil de reconocer que la de las criaturas? La historia de las grandes obras de arte arranca de los orígenes de la vida, se ha formado durante la vida del artista, y las generaciones ulteriores son esencialmente las que le confieren una supervivencia duradera. Cuando se manifiesta esta supervivencia, toma el nombre de fama. Las traducciones que son algo más que comunicaciones surgen cuando una obra sobrevive y alcanza la época de su fama. Por consiguiente, las traducciones no son las que prestan un servicio a la obra, como pretenden los malos traductores, sino que más bien deben a la obra su existencia. La vida del original alcanza en ellas su expansión póstuma más vasta y siempre renovada.

Paragraph 5 Chinese (Chen 2005: 5)

一种特殊的和高级的生命形式的展开过程也受到一种特殊的、高级的目的性所制约。生命与目的性之间的关系，看似明显然而几乎超越智力的掌握，只有在生命的所有个别目的性所趋向的终极目的不是在其自身领域而是在更高的领域里得以探讨时，才显示自身。生命的一切目的性显示，包括其自身的目的性，归根结底不在于生命，而在于生命本质的表达，在于其含义的再现。因此翻译最终为满足我们的需要而达到表现语言间内部关系的目的。它不可能揭示或确立这种隐藏的关系本身，但却可以通过胚胎的或强化的形式实现这种关系而将其再现。试图在胚胎中加以确立的尝试意指某事物，对这种事物的再现具有如此独特的性质，以至于在非语言生活领城极少遭遇得到。在其类比和象征中，它可以依赖其他方式暗示意义，而非强化的——即预见性的、暗示的——实现。至于假定的语言间的内在亲缘性，则以一种特殊的趋同性为标志。这种特殊的亲缘性是站得住脚的，因为各种语言绝不是相互陌生的，而是先验地、除了所有历史关系之外而在它们所表达的东西上相互关联的。

Pinyin romanization:

yī zhǒng tè shū de hé gāo jí de shēng mìng xíng shì de zhǎn kāi guò chéng yě shòu dào yī zhǒng tè shū de 、gāo jí de mù de xìng suǒ zhì yuē 。shēng mìng yǔ mù de xìng zhī jiān de guān xì ， kàn sì míng xiǎn rán ér jī hū chāo yuè zhì lì de zhǎng wò ， zhī yǒu zài shēng mìng de suǒ yǒu gè bié mù de xìng suǒ qū xiàng de zhōng jí mù de bú shì zài qí zì shēn lǐng yù ér shì zài gèng gāo de lǐng yù lǐ dé yǐ tàn tǎo shí ， cái xiǎn shì zì shēn 。shēng mìng de yī qiē mù de xìng xiǎn shì ， bāo kuò qí zì shēn de mù de xìng ， guī gēn jié dǐ bú zài yú shēng mìng ， ér zài yú shēng mìng běn zhì de biǎo dá ， zài yú qí hán yì de zài xiàn 。yīn cǐ fān yì zuì zhōng wéi mǎn zú wǒ men de xū yào ér dá dào biǎo xiàn yǔ yán jiān nèi bù guān xì de mù de 。tā bú kě néng jiē shì huò què lì zhè zhǒng yǐn cáng de guān xì běn shēn， dàn què kě yǐ tōng guò pēi tāi de huò qiáng huà de xíng shì shí xiàn zhè zhǒng guān xì ér jiāng qí zài xiàn。shì tú zài pēi tāi zhōng jiā yǐ què lì de cháng shì yì zhǐ mǒu shì wù， duì zhè zhǒng shì wù de zài xiàn jù yǒu rú cǐ dú tè de xìng zhì， yǐ zhì yú zài fēi yǔ yán shēng huó lǐng chéng jí shǎo zāo yù dé dào。zài qí lèi bǐ hé xiàng zhēng zhōng， tā kě yǐ yī lài qí tā fāng shì àn shì yì yì， ér fēi qiáng huà de——jí yù jiàn xìng de、àn shì de——shí xiàn。zhì yú jiǎ dìng de yǔ yán jiān de nèi zài qīn yuán xìng， zé yǐ yī zhǒng tè shū de qū tóng xìng wéi biāo zhì。zhè zhǒng tè shū de qīn yuán xìng shì zhàn dé zhù jiǎo de， yīn wéi gè zhǒng yǔ yán jué bú shì xiàng hù mò shēng de， ér shì xiān yàn dì、chú le suǒ yǒu lì shǐ guān xì zhī wài ér zài tā men suǒ biǎo dá de dōng xī shàng xiàng hù guān lián de。

Paragraph 6 Finnish (Lehto 1991/2007: 42–44)

Tämä selitysyritys näyttäisi kuitenkin palauttavan tarkastelun tarpeettomien kiertoteiden jälkeen takaisin perinteiseen käännösteoriaan. Jos käännösten tehtävänä on todistaa kielten sisäistä sukulaisuutta, miten muutoin ne voisivat siitä suoriutua kuin välittämällä mahdollisimman tarkasti alkuteoksen muodon ja sisällön? Mainittu teoria ei kuitenkaan ole kyennyt tekemään selkoa tämän tarkkuuden käsitteestä eikä niin muodoin perimmältään osoittamaan, mikä käännöksissä on oleellista. Tosiasiassa kielten sukulaisuus ilmeneekin käännöksessä paljon syvemmin ja täsmällisemmin kuin kahden runoelman pinnallisena ja määrittelemättömänä samanlaisuutena. Alkuteoksen ja käännöksen todellisen suhteen ymmärtämiseksi voimme turvautua argumenttiin, joka kärjeltään täysin vastaa tiedonkriitiikissä heijastusteorian mahdottomuuden osoittamiseksi käytettyjä ajatuskulkuja. Kuten jälkimmäisessä osoitetaan, että tiedon objektiivisuus ja sellaiseen pyrkiminenkin olisi mahdotonta, jos tämä ymmärretään jonkin todellisen heijastumaksi, voimme tässä väittää, että jos käännös olemukseltaan tähtäisi samankaltaisuuteen alkuteoksen kanssa, kääntäminen ei ylipäätään olisi mahdollista. Alkuteoksen elämän jatkuminen – niin kuin itse sanakin osoittaa – merkitsee nimittäin sen lakkaamatonta muuttumista ja uudistumista. Lopullisimmatkin sananvalinnat muuttuvat ja kypsyvät edelleen ajan myötä. Jokin mikä aikanaan ehkä oli vain idullaan oleva mahdollisuus runoilijan kielessä, voi myöhemmin kuulostaa kuluneelta; tietyt sanavalinnat voivat sitten saattaa liikkeelle kielen immanentteja tendenssejä. Jokin aikanaan tuoreelta tuntunut voi myöhemmin kuulostaa kuluneelta, aikanaan jokapäiväinen vaikuttaa arkaaiselta. Tällaisten muutosten – kuin myös yhtä lailla lakkaamattomien merkityssiirtymien – olemuksen hakeminen jälkipolvien subjektiviteetista kielen ja kieliluomien elämän sijasta merkitsisi jo alkeellisimmankin psykologismin valossa paitsi syyn ja seurauksen sekoittamista, myös ja ennen muuta suunnattomien ja tavattoman hedelmällisten historiallisten prosessien sivuuttamista silkan henkisen laiskuuden vuoksi. Ja vaikka kirjailijan viimeinen kynänveto joskus onnistuttaisiinkin osoittamaan hänen teoksensa kulmakiveksi, tämäkään ei vielä pelastaisi kyseistä kuollutta käännösteoriaa. Sillä niin kuin suurten runoelmien sävyt ja sisällöt vuosisatojen saatossa muuttuvat tykkänään toisiksi, niin muuttuu myös kääntäjän äidinkieli. Niin on upeimmankin käännöksen osana yhtä aikaa antaa panoksensa oman kielensä kasvuun ja luhistua sen muutoksessa. Niin kauas käännös jää tyhjästä samuudesta kahden kuolleen kielen välillä, että kaikista taidemuodoista juuri sen osaksi laukeaa osoittaa niin vieraitten sanojen jälkituleentumista kuin omien poltteita.

References

Attridge, Derek. 1988. "Unpacking the Portmanteau, or Who's Afraid of *Finnegans Wake*?" In Jonathan Culler, ed., *On Puns: The Foundation of Letters*, 140–55. Oxford: Blackwell.

Barthes, Roland. 1968. "La mort de l'auteur." Source text of Howard 1967. *Mantéia* 5.

Benjamin, Roy. 2013. "Noirse-Made-Earsy: Noise in *Finnegans Wake*." *Comparative Literature Studies* 50.4: 670–87.

Benjamin, Walter. 1923/1972. "Die Aufgabe des Übersetzers." In Tillman Rexroth, ed., *Kleine Prosa, Baudelaire-Übertragungen* (Short Prose, Baudelaire Transpositions), 9–21. Vol. 4, Part 1 of Walter Benjamin, *Gesammelte Schriften* (Collected Writings). Frankfurt am Main: Suhrkamp.

Bergvall, Caroline. 2000. "VIA (48 Dante Variations)." https://writing.upenn.edu/~afilreis/88v/bergvall-via.html. Accessed August 5, 2023.

Berman, Antoine. 2008/2018. *The Age of Translation: A Commentary on Walter Benjamin's "The Task of the Translator."* Translated and with an introduction by Chantal Wright. London, UK, and New York, NY: Routledge.

Broda, Martine, trans. 1991. Walter Benjamin, "La tâche du traducteur." Translation of Benjamin 1923/1972. *Po&sie* 55: 150–58. https://po-et-sie.fr/wp-content/uploads/2018/10/551991p150158.pdf. Accessed May 12, 2023.

Cadbury, Bill. 2007. "The March of a Maker: Chapters 1.2–4." In Luca Crispi and Sam Slote, eds., *How Joyce Wrote Finnegans Wake: A Chapter-by-Chapter Genetic Guide*, 66–97. Madison: University of Wisconsin Press.

陈永国 (Chen Yongguo), trans. 2005. 瓦尔特·本雅明 (Walter Benjamin), 译者的任务 (The Task of the Translator). Translation of Benjamin 1923/1972. In Chen Yongguo, ed. and trans., 《翻译与后现代性》 (Translation and Postmodernity), 3–12. Beijing: 中国人民大学出版社 (China Renmin University Press).

Chrisp, Peter. 2016. "Who is Dreaming Finnegans Wake?" *From Swerve of Shore to Bend of Bay* 6 (June 20). http://peterchrisp.blogspot.com/2016/06/who-is-dreaming-finnegans-wake.html. Accessed May 20, 2023.

Chrisp, Peter. 2017. "Edgar Quinet in Finnegans Wake." *From Swerve of Shore to Bend of Bay* 7 (July 28). http://peterchrisp.blogspot.com/2017/07/edgar-quinet-in-finnegans-wake.html. Accessed April 30, 2023.

Cohen, Sharmila, and Paul Legault, eds. 2012. *The Sonnets: Translating and Rewriting Shakespeare*. New York: Nightboat.

Collins, Martha, and Kevin Prufer, ed. 2017. *Into English: Poems, Translations, Commentaries*. Minneapolis: Graywolf.

Damrosch, David. 2003. *What is World Literature?* Princeton and Oxford: Princeton University Press.

Dash, Michael, trans. 1992. Edouard Glissant, *Caribbean Discourse*. Translation of Glissant 1997. Charlottesville: University Press of Virginia.

Derrida, Jacques. 1985. "Des Tours de Babel." In Joseph F. Graham, ed., *Difference in Translation*, 165–205 (in English, translated by Joseph F. Graham) and 209–48 (in French). Ithaca, NY: Cornell University Press.

Ellmann, Richard. 1959/1982. *James Joyce*. Oxford and New York: Oxford University Press.

Ferreira, Duarte, João. 1995. "The Power of Babel: 'Pure Language' as Intertranslation." *Perspectives: Studies in Translatology* 3.2: 271–82.

Foucault, Michel. 1969/1983. "Qu'est-ce qu'un auteur?" *littoral* 9 (June): 3–32.

Glissant, Edouard. 1981. *Le discours antillais*. Paris: Seuil.

Gómez, Alcántara, and Guillermo Alejandro, trans. 1971. Walter Benjamin, "La tarea del traductor." Translation of Benjamin 1923/1972. In Walter Benjamin, *Angelus Novus*, 127–43. Barcelona: Edhasa.

Gore, Thomas, Alice Jardine, and Leon S. Roudiez, trans. 1980a. Julia Kristeva, *Desire in Language: A Semiotic Approach to Literature and Art*. Edited by Leon S. Roudiez. New York: Columbia University Press.

Gore, Thomas, Alice Jardine, and Leon S. Roudiez, trans. 1980b. Julia Kristeva, "The Bounded Text." Translation of Kristeva 1968. In Gore et al. 1980a: 36–63.

Gore, Thomas, Alice Jardine, and Leon S. Roudiez, trans. 1980c. Julia Kristeva, "Word, Dialogue and Novel." Translation of Kristeva 1967. In Gore et al. 1980a: 64–91.

Groys, Boris. 2016. "The Truth of Art." *E-flux* 71 (March). www.e-flux.com/journal/71/60513/the-truth-of-art/. Accessed May 22, 2023.

Halpern, Daniel, ed. 1993. *Dante's Inferno*. New York: Ecco.

Hart, Clive. 1962. *Structure and Motif in* Finnegans Wake. Evanston: Northwestern University Press.

Hermans, Theo. 1996. "The Translator's Voice in Translated Narrative." *Target* 8.1: 23–48.

Hofstadter, Douglas. 1997. *Le ton beau de Marot: In Praise of the Music of Language*. New York: Basic.

Howard, Richard, trans. 1967. Roland Barthes, "The Death of the Author." Translation of Barthes 1968. *Aspen* 5-6.3: 2–6.

Joyce, James. 1939/1975. *Finnegans Wake*. London: Faber & Faber. Abbreviated *FW* in the text.

Jung, Carl Gustav. 1952/1975. "'Ulysses': A Monologue." In Herbert Read, Michael Fordham, Gerhard Adler, and William McGuire, eds., *The Spirit in Man, Art, and Literature*, 117–34. Vol. 15 of *The Collected Works of C.G. Jung*. Translated by R.F.C. Hull. Princeton: Princeton University Press.

Kaplan, Robert. 2002. "Madness and James Joyce." *Australasian Psychiatry* 10.2: 172–76.

Kitcher, Philip. 2009. *Joyce's Kaleidoscope: An Invitation to* Finnegans Wake. Oxford and New York: Oxford University Press.

Kenner, Hugh. 1987. *Dublin's Joyce*. New York: Columbia University Press.

Kristeva, Julia. 1967. "Le mot, le dialogue et le roman." *Critique Critique* 23.239 (April): 438–65.

Kristeva, Julia. 1968. "Le texte clos." *Linguistique et littérature, sous la direction de Roland Barthes*, Special Issue of *Langages* 3.12: 103–25.

Lacan, Jacques. 2005. *Le Sinthome*. Paris: Seuil.

Lehto, Leevi, trans. 1991/2007. Walter Benjamin, "Kääntäjän tehtävä" (The Translator's Task). Translation of Benjamin 1923/1972. In Tapani Kilpeläinen, ed., *Kääntökirja: Kirjoituksia kääntämisen filosofiasta* (Turn Book: Writings on the Philosophy of Translation), 39–52. Tampere: niin & näin/European Philosophy Society.

Lethem, Jonathan. 2007. "The Ecstasy of Influence: A Plagiarism." *Harper's Magazine*. https://harpers.org/archive/2007/02/the-ecstasy-of-influence/. Accessed November 2, 2021.

Liska, Vivian. 2014. "A Same Other, Another Same: Walter Benjamin and Maurice Blanchot on Translation." Translated by Naomi Shulman. *German Quarterly* 87.2 (Spring): 229–45.

Liu, Lydia H. 1999. "The Question of Meaning-Value in the Political Economy of the Sign." In Liu, ed., *Tokens of Exchange: The Problem of Translation in Global Circulations*, 13–41. Durham: Duke University Press.

Lukes, Alexandra, ed. 2023. *Avant-Garde Translation*. Leiden and Boston: Brill.

MacCabe, Colin. 1982/2016. "An Introduction to *Finnegans Wake*." In John Harty III, ed., *James Joyce's* Finnegans Wake*: A Casebook*, 23–32. London and New York: Routledge.

Malmkjær, Kirsten. 1988. "Cooperation and Literary Translation." In Leo Hickey, ed., *The Pragmatics of Translation*, 25–40. Clevedon: Multilingual Matters.

Marx, Karl. 1939. *Grundrisse der Kritik der politischen Ökonomie.* Moscow: Institute for Marxism-Leninism. http://dhcm.inkrit.org/wp-content/data/mew42.pdf. Accessed May 7, 2023.

McEwen, Cameron. 2017. "Bellum-Pax-Bellum." *McLuhan's New Sciences* 10. https://mcluhansnewsciences.com/mcluhan/2017/10/bellum-pax-bellum/. Accessed May 1, 2023.

McKay, Becka Mara. 2011. "20 More 'Rules': Becka McKay on Teaching Translation and Petra Dünges on Translating Picture Books." *Arab Lit & Arab Lit Quarterly* (September 8). https://arablit.org/2011/09/08/20-more-rules-becka-mckay-on-teaching-translation-and-petra-dunges-on-translating-picture-books/. Accessed August 5, 2023.

Melnick, David. 1983. *Men in Aida*, Book One. *Tuumba* 47. http://eclipsearchive.org/projects/TUUMBA/TUUMBA47/Tuumba47.pdf. Accessed June 26, 2019.

Melnick, David. 2015. *Men in Aida*. The Hague and Tirana: Uitgeverij.

Nakayasu, Sawako. 2011. *Mouth: Eats Color: Sagawa Chika Translations, Anti-Translations, & Originals.* Providence: Factorial.

Nicolaus, Martin, trans. 1973. Karl Marx, *Grundrisse: Foundations of the Critique of Political Economy.* Translation of Marx 1939. Harmondsworth: Penguin. www.marxists.org/archive/marx/works/1857/grundrisse/. Accessed May 7, 2023.

Noel, Urayoán. 2021. *Transversal*. Tucson: University of Arizona Press.

O'Neill, Patrick. 2005. *Polyglot Joyce*. Toronto: University of Toronto Press.

O'Neill, Patrick 2013. *Impossible Joyce: Finnegans Wakes.* Toronto: University of Toronto Press.

O'Neill, Patrick. 2022. *Finnegans Wakes: Tales of Translation.* Toronto: University of Toronto Press.

Pavlov, Evgeny. n.d. "Задача переводчика" (*Zadacha perevodchika*/The Task of the Translator). Translation of Benjamin 1923/1972. http://kassandrion.narod.ru/commentary/11/6ben.htm. Accessed May 8, 2023.

Price, A.R., trans. 2016. Jacques Lacan, *The Sinthome: The Seminar of Jacques Lacan, Book XXIII.* Translation of Lacan 2005. Edited by Jacques-Alain Miller. Cambridge, UK, and Malden, MA: Polity.

Pym, Anthony. 1993. "Performatives as a Key to Modes of Translational Discourse." In János Kohn and Klinga Klaudy, eds., *Transferre necesse est ... Current Issues in Translation Theory*, 47–62. Szombathely, Hungary: Pädagogische Hochschule Berzsenyi Dániel.

Reiss, Katharina. 1981. "Type, Kind and Individuality of Text: Decision Making in Translation." In *Translation Theory and Intercultural Relations*, special issue of *Poetics Today* 2.4 (Autumn): 121–31. www.jstor.org/stable/1772491. Accessed July 19, 2023. https://doi.org/10.2307/1772491.

Riley, Brendan. 2023. "The Fluid Dynamics of Authorial Identity: On Douglas Robinson's *The Last Days of Maiju Lassila* and His Transcreation of Volter

Kilpi's *Gulliver's Voyage to Phantomimia*." *Los Angeles Review of Books* (February 13). https://lareviewofbooks.org/article/the-fluid-dynamics-of-authorial-identity-on-douglas-robinsons-the-last-days-of-maiju-lassila-and-his-transcreation-of-volter-ki/. Accessed May 22, 2023.

Robert-Foley, Lily. 2020. "The Politics of Experimental Translation: Potentialities and Preoccupations." *English* 69.267: 401–19.

Robert-Foley, Lily. 2023. *Experimental Translation*. London: Goldsmiths.

Robinson, Douglas. 1997/2014. *Western Translation Theory from Herodotus to Nietzsche*. London and New York: Routledge.

Robinson, Douglas. 2003. *Performative Linguistics: Speaking and Translating as Doing Things With Words*. London and New York: Routledge.

Robinson, Douglas. 2017a. *Aleksis Kivi and/as World Literature*. Leiden and Boston: Brill.

Robinson, Douglas, trans. 2017b. Aleksis Kivi, *The Brothers Seven*. Bucharest: Zeta.

Robinson, Douglas. 2017c. *Critical Translation Studies*. London and Singapore: Routledge.

Robinson, Douglas. 2017d. *Translationality: Essays in the Medical-Translational Humanities*. London and New York: Routledge.

Robinson, Douglas. 2019. *Transgender, Translation, Translingual Address*. London and New York: Bloomsbury Academic.

Robinson, Douglas, trans. 2020. Volter Kilpi, *Gulliver's Voyage to Phantomimia*. Bucharest: Zeta.

Robinson, Douglas. 2021. "Sixteen Avant-Garde Perspectives on World Literature and the Translator's (In)visibility." *Asymptote* (January), Special Feature: "New World Literature." https://www.asymptotejournal.com/special-feature/sixteen-avantgarde-perspectives-on-world-literature-and-the-translators-invisibility-douglas-robinson/.

Robinson, Douglas. 2022a. "Heteronymous Narratoriality: The Translator (as Narrator) as Somebody Else." *Cultus* 15: 56–75.

Robinson, Douglas, pseudotrans. 2022b. J I Vatanen, *The Last Days of Maiju Lassila*. Austin, TX: Atmosphere.

Robinson, Douglas. 2022c. *The Strange Loops of Translation*. London and New York: Bloomsbury Academic.

Robinson, Douglas. 2023a. "An Alphabet of Avant-Garde Perspectives on World Literature and the Translator's (In)visibility: With an Avant-Garde Translation of Walter Benjamin's 'Die Aufgabe des Übersetzers'." *Lukes* 2023: 201–40.

Robinson, Douglas. 2023b. *The Behavioral Economics of Translation*. London and New York: Routledge.

Robinson, Douglas. 2023c. *The Experimental Translator*. London and New York: Palgrave Macmillan.

Robinson, Douglas. 2023d. *Questions for Translation Studies*. Amsterdam and Philadelphia: John Benjamins.

Robinson, Douglas. 2023e. *Translation as a Form: A Centennial Commentary on Walter Benjamin's "The Task of the Translator*." London and New York: Routledge.

Robinson, Douglas. 2024a. *Insecticide: A Republican Romance*. Austin, TX: Atmosphere.

Robinson, Douglas. 2024b. *Translator, Touretter: Avant-Garde Translation and the Touretter Sublime*. Leiden and Boston: Brill.

Robinson, Douglas, trans. Forthcoming, 2025. "Walter Benjamin's 'D'oof-gobble Dusk Over Seltzers'." In Delphine Grass and Lily Robert-Foley, eds., *The Unending Lives of Translation: Creative-Critical Experiments in Translation and Life Writing*. London: UCL Press.

Robinson, Douglas, and Xiaorui Sun. Forthcoming, 2025. *Translation, Pornography, Performativity: Experimenting with That Dangerous Supplement*. London and New York: Routledge.

Rouse, Howard. 2020. "*Finnegans Wake*: A Dream of Joyce—and its Real." *Lacanian Review Online* 264 (December 13): n.p. www.thelacanianreviews.com/finnegans-wake-a-dream-of-joyce-and-its-real/. Accessed July 19, 2023.

Saunders, Max. 2010. *Self Impression: Life-Writing, Autobiografiction, and the Forms of Modern Literature*. Oxford and New York: Oxford University Press.

Schiavi, Giuliana. 1996. "There Is Always a Teller in a Tale." *Target* 8.1: 1–21.

Schlossmann, Beryl. 2017. "Mirrors/ Lacan with Joyce/ Theory, Psychoanalysis, and Literature." https://breac.nd.edu/articles/mirrors-lacan-with-joyce-theory-psychoanalysis-and-literature/. *Breac: A Digital Journal of Irish Studies* (July 27): n.p.. Accessed July 19, 2023.

Scott, Clive. 2012a. *Literary Translation and the Rediscovery of Reading*. Cambridge, UK: Cambridge University Press.

Scott, Clive. 2012b. *Translating the Perception of Text*. Oxford, UK: Legenda.

Scott, Clive. 2018. *The Work of Literary Translation*. Cambridge, UK, and New York: Cambridge University Press.

Sedgwick, Eve. 2003. *Touching Feeling: Affect, Pedagogy, Performativity*. Durham: Duke University Press.

Senn, Fritz. 1970. "*Ulysses* in Translation." In Thomas F. Staley and Bernard Benstock, eds., *Approaches to Ulysses: Ten Essays*, 249–86. Pittsburgh: University of Pittsburgh Press.

Senn, Fritz. 1978. "'Entzifferungen und Proben': *Finnegans Wake* in der Brechung von Arno Schmidt" (Decipherings and Assays: *FW* in Arno Schmidt's Breaking/Broaching/Transmutation). *Bargfelder Bote* 27 (February): 3–14.

Senn, Fritz. 1993. "'Wehg' zu Finnegan? Dieter Stündel's Ubertragung von *Finnegans Wake*" ("Woe/[A]way" to Finnegan? Dieter Stündel's Transposition of *FW*). *Neue Zürcher Zeitung* (July 10-11): 59–60.

Senn, Fritz. 1998. "'ALP Deutsch': Ob überhaupt möglich?" (ALP in German: Even Possible?). In Karen R. Lawrence, ed., *Transcultural Joyce*, 187–92. Cambridge: Cambridge University Press.

Senn, Fritz. 2013. "How James Joyce Translates Himself." *Cahier de l'ILSL* 38: 123–37.

Shell, Marc. 1982. *Money, Language, and Thought: Literary and Philosophic Economies from the Medieval to the Modern Era*. Berkeley and Los Angeles: University of California Press.

Stündel, Dieter H., trans. 1993. James Joyce, *Finnegans Wehg*. Translation of Joyce 1939/1975. Darmstadt: Häusser and Frankfurt am Main: Zweitausendeins.

Sun, Xiaorui. 2023. "Rethinking the Theoretical Underpinnings of Translation Studies: Re-fathoming Normative Translation Studies as Experimental." *Journal of Translation Studie*.

Thirlwell, Adam, ed. 2012. "Multiples: 12 Stories in 18 Languages by 61 Authors." *McSweeny's* 42. https://store.mcsweeneys.net/products/mcsweeneys-issue-42. Accessed August 12, 2023.

Tindall, William York. 1959. *A Reader's Guide to James Joyce*. New York: Noonday.

Ullman, Alexander. 2018. "The Sound of Translation: Joyce, the Zukofskys, and Liturgical *Piyutim*." *Partial Answers: Journal of Literature and the History of Ideas* 16.1 (January): 43–64.

van Rooten, Luis-d'Antin. 1967. *Mots D'Heures: Gousses, Rames*. New York: Viking.

Venuti, Lawrence, ed. 2012. *The Translation Studies Reader*. London and New York: Routledge.

Waldrop, Rosemarie, ed. 2000. *Reft and Light*. Providence: Burning Deck.

Weinberger, Eliot. 1987. *Nineteen Ways of Looking at Wang Wei*. New York: New Directions.

Zukofsky, Celia T., and Louis, trans. 1969. *Catullus (Gai Valeri Catulli Veronensis liber)*. London: Cape Goliard.

Index

Note: References to notes are provided as the page number followed by "n" and the note number, e.g. 22n3 refers to note 3 on page 22.

Asymptote 61
Attridge, Derek 26
Aubert, Jacques 22n3
"Aufgabe des Übersetzers, Die" (Benjamin) 28, 43, 53, 59–61, 62n5, 64, 82, 111, 112n1
Author-function (Foucault) 107
Avant-Garde Translation (Lukes) 61

Barthes, Roland 105, 107, 116n3
Baudelaire, Charles 80n13
"Bellum-Pax-Bellum" (McEwen) 7
Benjamin, Roy 31
Benjamin, Walter 43, 45, 60–63, 65n1, 66n3, 67n4, 70n7, 87n29; and etymological literalism 28, 60, 111; macrotext of 111–13, 115
"Benjamins Totin' Vodka" (Robinson) 28, 45, 59–60, 64, 65–103, 113, 115, 119, 121
Bergvall, Caroline 117–18n4
Berman, Antoine 66n3, 87–88n29
Borromean knot (Lacan) 42–43
Broda, Martine 66n3, 67n4, 121
Brothers Seven, The (Kivi/Robinson) 85n25
Brunt, Captain Samuel 54
"Buckley and the Russian General" (Joyce) 5, 9n3
Budgen, Frank 11

Cage, John 108
Capital (Marx) 39
Cartwright, Ethel (Kilpi) 55
Catullus (Zukofskys) 23
Cervantes, Miguel Saavedra de 114
Cézanne, Paul 34
Chen, Yongguo 74n9, 76n10, 124
Chomsky, Noam 26–27n5
Chrisp, Peter 7, 52
Cicero, Marcus Tullius 22–23n4
Civilisation et les grands fleuves historiques, La (Metchnikoff) 7
Clancy, George 108
Coach with the Six Insides (Erdman) 108
Cohen, Sharmila 117–18n4
Collins, Martha 117–18n4
Copernican Hypothesis (Kant) 116n3
Coscienza di Zeno, La (Svevo) 50
Critical Translation Studies (Robinson) 37

Damrosch, David 117–18n4
Dante Alighieri 114
Dash, Michael 25
De optimo genere oratorum (Cicero) 22–23n4
Dedalus, Stephen (Joyce) 47, 49–50
DeepL 29, 112
Deleuze, Gilles 33, 115

Derrida, Jacques 33
Descriptive Translation Studies 59
Dilthey, Wilhelm 63, 71n8
Discourse of the hysteric (Lacan) 16
Djoytsch (Hart) 10, 13, 32
Djreamish 5–6, 9, 10n4, 13–16, 18, 21, 27, 30, 32–33, 39–41, 45, 51–53, 63–64, 65n1, 70n6, 72, 79, 94, 97
Dryden, John 22–23n4
Dubliners (Joyce) 19, 47, 50

Ecstasy (Longinus) 9
"Ecstasy of Influence, The" (Lethem) 9
"Edgar Quinet in Finnegans Wake" (Chrisp) 7
Ellmann, Richard 7
Erdman, Jean 108
Esau (Genesis) 32
Etymology: and Joycean research 2; and Hölderlinian literalism 28, 60, 62, 111
Experimental Translation (Robert-Foley) 61, 113
Experimental translation 5, 8–9, 14, 16–20, 58, 104, 117, 120; of Benjamin 28, 61–62, 64, 65–103, 111–12; and heteronyms 53, 59; in Joyce 10, 13–14, 25; of Marx 41; and metatextuality (O'Neill) 105; and psychosis (Lacan) 17, 45–46
Experimental Translator, The (Robinson) 9, 53

Fagles, Robert 22–23n4
Ferreira Duarte, João 66n3
"Finigan's Wake" 5, 18–19, 64
"Finnegans Wake: A Dream of Joyce—and its Real" (Rouse) 41–42
Finnegans Wakes (O'Neill) 18n1, 107
Finnegans Wehg (Joyce/Stündel) 60
Foucault, Michel 16, 107
Fouéré, Olwen 108
Freud, Sigmund 34, 96n56
Frost, Robert 2

Gellius, Aulus 10–11
Glissant, Édouard 25
Goethe, Johann Wolfgang von 107, 114
Gogarty, Oliver St. John 108–9
Gómez Alcántara, Guillermo Alejandro 70n6, 71n8, 123
"Grammatically extended neotranslation" (Outranspo) 29
Groys, Boris 58
Grundrisse (Marx) 39
Guattari, Félix 115
Gulliver, Lemuel 54–56, 113n2
Gulliver's Voyage to Phantomimia (Kilpi/Robinson) 53, 113n2

Halley, Edmund 54
Halpern, Daniel 117–18n4
Hart, Clive 9, 10n4, 11, 13n5
Herder, J.G. von 6
Hermans, Theo 59
Heterolingual address (Sakai) 39
Heteronyms 29, 51–60, 62; in "Benjamins Totin' Vodka" 63–64, 65n1, 112–13; coined by Pessoa 47–48, 52
Hofstadter, Douglas 117–18n4
Hölderlin, Friedrich 84; and etymological literalism 28, 60, 62, 111; and psychosis 43–45; and Romanticism 87–88n29
Homer 22–23n4, 108, 114, 116n3
Homophonic translation 30, 37; of Benjamin 28–29, 60–64, 65n1, 66n3, 67n5; 112–13; in Joyce 21–22, 25, 27; serial 27, 27, 29, 37, 63, 65–79, 113
"How Joyce Translates Himself" (Senn) 19
Howard, Richard 105

Ideen zu Philosophie der Geschichte der Menschheit (Herder) 6
Impossible Joyce (O'Neill) 107

Insecticide (Robinson) 9n2, 53
Intertextuality (Kristeva) 105
"Invention of the Real, The" (Lacan/ Miller) 41
Isaac (Genesis) 32

Jacob (Genesis) 32
James Joyce Centre 110
Jerome, St 22–23n4
"Joyce the Symptom" (Lacan) 22n3, 41
Joyce Tower Museum 110
Judaeus, Philo 70n7, 80n13

"Kääntäjän tehtävä" (Benjamin/ Lehto) 29, 76n10, 79n11, 125–26
Kant, Immanuel 87–88n29, 116n3
Kenner, Hugh 52
Kilpi, Volter 53–55
Kirkus reviews 56
Kitcher, Philip 14, 52–53
Kivi, Aleksis 85n25
Kristeva, Julia 105, 116n3

"Lac, Le" (Lamartine) 35
Lacan, Jacques 13, 16, 22n3, 33, 41–43, 45–46, 66, 96n56
Lamartine, Alphonse de 35
Lassila, Maiju (Untola, Vatanen/ Robinson) 53, 56–57, 113
Last Days of Maiju Lassila, The (Vatanen/Robinson) 53, 113n2
Legault, Paul 117–18n4
Lehto, Leevi 29, 76n10, 79n11, 112, 125
Lethem, Jonathan 8–9
Lewis, Wyndham 55
Liang Siting, Stella 17
Liska, Vivian 66n3
Littoral translation 25
Liu, Lydia H. 37–38, 41
Longinus 9
Lukes, Alexandra 61

Macrotextual reading (O'Neill) 106–8, 110–13, 115, 116n3, 117
Mallarmé, Stêphane 63
Malmkjær, Kirsten 57
Martello Tower 108
Marx, Karl 37–39, 41
Massumi, Brian 115
McEwen, Cameron 7
McKay, Becca Mara 117–18n4
Melnick, David 27
Merleau-Ponty, Maurice 34
Metatextual reading (O'Neill) 105–6, 111, 116
Metchnikoff, Léon 7, 13
Minton, Phil 108
Mise en abîme 12–13, 50–51
Motherless Brooklyn (Lethem) 9
Mouthfull of Ecstasy (Minton) 108
Mulligan, Buck 109
Museo Joyce Trieste 110

Nabokov, Vladimir 55
Nakayasu, Sawako 117–18n4
Nicolaus, Martin 37–39, 41
Noel, Urajoán 25
"Nominal identities as ready-mades" (Groys) 58

O'Neill, Patrick 18, 104–8, 110–12, 114–17
Odyssey (Homer) 108
"Oof-gobble Dusk Over Seltzers, D'" (Benjamin/Robinson) 61, 112–13, 115
Outranspo 21, 29
Overwriting (Scott) 16n6, 34–35

Pale Fire (Nabokov) 55
Pannwitz, Rudolf 63
"Panther, Der" (Rilke) 36
Pavlov, Evgeny 67n5, 70n6, 122
Periperformativity (Sedgwick) 58
Pessoa, Fernando 47–49, 52
Piyutim 21, 23
Pliny 7, 10–11
Polyglot Joyce (O'Neill) 104
Portmanteau words (Joyce) 1, 29–32, 37, 42, 60, 62; in "Benjamins Totin' Vodka" 64, 65n1, 79n11, 113; in Hart 10n4, 13n5, 32; in *Insecticide* 9n2; the self as 48; translouting into

32, 37–41; read by Ullman as "smashing words" 26–27, 30
Portrait of the Artist as a Young Man, A (Joyce) 19, 47–50, 109
Pound, Ezra 55
Preface to Ovid's Epistles (Dryden) 22–23n4
Price, A.R. 42
Prototextual reading (O'Neill) 104, 106, 108, 111, 114–15, 116n3, 118–19; anti- 116
Proust, Marcel 107, 114
Prufer, Kevin 117–18n4
Pseudotranslation (Toury) 56
Psychosis, in Hölderlin (Benjamin) 44–45; in Joyce (Lacan) 43, 45; in translating 45–46
Pym, Anthony 57

Questions for Translation Studies (Robinson) 53
Quinet, Edgar 6–13, 23, 37

Reading: macrotextual (O'Neill) 106–8, 110–13, 115, 116n3, 117; metatextual (O'Neill) 105–6, 111, 116; prototextual (O'Neill) 104, 106, 108, 111, 114–15, 116n3, 118–19; stereoscopic 117; transtextual (O'Neill) 107, 117–20
Reader-response criticism 116n3
Readerly text (Barthes) 105
Reiß, Katharina 33
Rezeptionsästhetik 116n3
Rhizomaticity (Deleuze/Guattari) 115
Riley, Brendan 57n3
Rilke, Rainer Maria 36
riverrun (Fouéré) 108
"Road Not Taken, The" (Frost) 2
Roaratorio (Cage) 108
Robert-Foley, Lily 21, 25, 61–62, 113
Rouse, Howard 41–43

Sakai, Naoki 39
Saunders, Max 47–51
Schiavi, Giuliana 59
Schlossmann, Beryl 42n7
Scott, Clive 16n6, 34–37
Scotus, Duns 63
Sedgwick, Eve 58
Self Impression (Saunders) 47
Seminar XXIII: Le/The Sinthome (Lacan) 16, 41–42
Senn, Fritz 4, 10, 18–21, 23, 27, 41
Serial: homophonic translation 21, 27, 29, 37, 63, 65–79, 113; literalism 29; DeepL translation 29; proliferation of readings (O'Neill) 34, 37, 106; translation of Quinet 37
Shakespeare, William 107
Shaw Weaver, Harriet 13, 30–31
Shell, Marc 37, 41
Sinn Féin 109
Sinthome (Lacan) 43, 45; *see also Seminar XXIII*
Sinthome, The (Lacan/Miller) 16
Skin of Our Teeth, The (Wilder) 108
Sonotranslation (Outranspo) 21, 25, 29, 121; *see also Homophonic translation, Translauting*
"Sound of Translation: Joyce, the Zukofskys, and Liturgical *Piyutim*" (Ullman) 22
Stephen Hero (Joyce) 50
"Stopping by Woods on a Snowy Evening" (Frost) 2
Stündel, Dieter H. 60
Sun, Xiaorui 80n13
Surrealism 16n6
Svevo, Italo 50
Swift, Jonathan 54–56

Text-type theory (Reiß) 33
TG-grammar (Chomsky) 26–27n5
Thirlwell, Adam 117–18n4
Tindall, William York 50
Tolstoy, Leo 114
"Tours de Babel, Des" (Derrida) 20
Tower of Babel 23
Translating the Perception of Text (Scott) 16n6, 34

Translation as a Form (Robinson) 60–62, 66n3
Translation Studies Reader (Venuti) 22–23n4
Translation: of Benjamin 28–29, 60–64, 65n1, 66n3, 67n5; 112–13; homophonic 30, 37; in Joyce 21–22, 25, 27; littoral 25; sense-for-sense 22–24, 28, 60, 111; word-for-word 22, 24
Translation, Pornography, Performativity (Robinson/Sun) 80n13
Translator-function 107
Translator, Touretter (Robinson) 8, 53, 120
Translauting 63; as homophonic translating 24, 29, 60, 62, 64, 65n1, 66n3, 67n5, 70n6, 74n9, 76n10
Translouchewality 120
"Translout that gaswind into turfish" 2–4, 91; into djreamish 13–14, 16, 33, 45; in the *FW* context 6–7, 9–10, 79
Translouter 8, 69
Translouting 9, 18, 120; of Benjamin 62, 82, 99, 102–3; into portmanteau djreamish 32–33
Transtextual reading (O'Neill) 107, 117–20
Trench, Samuel Chenevix 109

Ullman, Alexander 22–27, 30
Ulysses (Joyce) 14–15, 19, 108–10; heteronyms in 47–48, 50
Unending Lives of Translation, The (Grass/Robert-Foley) 62
Untola, Algot 57
"Upgiving o' th' O'ersetter, Th'" (Benjamin/Robinson) 28, 61, 111–12, 115

van Rooten, Luis d'Antin 27
Vatanen, J.I. 53–54, 56–57
Venuti, Lawrence 22–23n4
Vico, Giambattista 7
Virgil 114
Voyage to Cacklogallinia, A (Brunt) 54
Vulgate translation of the Bible (Jerome) 22–23n4

Wake, The (Kvium/Lemmerz) 108
Waldrop, Rosemarie 117–18n4
Weinberger, Eliot 117–18n4
Western Translation Theory from Herodotus to Nietzsche (Robinson) 22–23n4
Wilder, Thornton 108
World literature 117

Zukofsky, Celia T. and Louis 23
Zusammenhang des Lebens (Dilthey/Benjamin) 71n8

For Product Safety Concerns and Information please contact our EU
representative GPSR@taylorandfrancis.com
Taylor & Francis Verlag GmbH, Kaufingerstraße 24, 80331 München, Germany

www.ingramcontent.com/pod-product-compliance
Lightning Source LLC
LaVergne TN
LVHW010924110826
845149LV00013B/2472

* 9 7 8 1 0 3 2 7 4 6 8 9 0 *